Manson's
BRISTOL MISCELLANY

Searching for the soul of the city

Michael Manson

VOLUME 1

   **Tangent** Books

Bristol Books CIC, The Courtyard, Wraxall,
Wraxall Hill, Bristol, BS48 1NA
www.bristolbooks.org

Tangent Books, Unit 5.16 Paintworks,
Bristol BS4 3EH
www.tangentbooks.co.uk

Manson's Bristol Miscellany: Volume I
Written and researched by Michael Manson

Published by Bristol Books 2021
in partnership with Tangent Books

ISBN: 9781909446267

Copyright: Michael Manson

Design: Joe Burt

Front cover illustration by Aga Kubish

Michael Manson has asserted his right under the Copyright, Designs and Patents Act of 1988 to be identified as the author of this work.

All rights reserved. This book may not be reproduced or transmitted in any form or in any means without the prior written consent of the publisher, except by a reviewer who wishes to quote brief passages in connection with a review written in a newspaper or magazine or broadcast on television, radio or on the internet.

A CIP record for this book is available from the British Library.

Any mistakes in this book are entirely the authors responsibility.
The author would be happy to correct them in any future prints of this book.

INTRODUCTION	7
IN THE BEGINNING	9

A few modest mounds
    Bristol's hill forts   9

What did the Romans do for Bristol?
    Abonae   11

A flourishing Community
    The Domesday Book   13

Water power
    Access to Important Trading Routes   14
    Bristol's Rivers, Streams and Brooks   15

POWER AND POLITICS   19

County Limits
    The County of Bristol   19

Easing the way to heaven
    Church and Chapel   21

St Anne's Holy Well
    Bristol's Holy Well   22

Islands in the Bristol Channel
    Steep Holm and Flat Holm   23

A meeting place at times of stress or celebration
    Bristol's High Cross   24

A castle, a ship, an eel and a fish
    Bristol's Coat of Arms   26

Where's the castle?
    Bristol Castle   27

The walls came tumbling down
    Walls and Gateways   29

Coining it
    The Mint   32

Really, very ugly
    The Mansion House   33

Who ordered the unicorns?
    City Hall   34

'What shadows we are, and what shadows we pursue'
    Edmund Burke 1729-97   37

The power behind the throne?
    Society of Merchant Venturers   38

LAW AND ORDER   41

An intriguing deterrent to prostitution
    The Courts   41

Brutal entertainment for harsh times
    Punishment   43

'A perfect command of temper'
    The policing of Bristol   47

PRISONS   51

Castles, gatehouses and dungeons
    Bristol's prisons   51
    Newgate Gaol   52
    Bridewell   52
    Lawford's Gate Gaol   53
    The New Gaol   53
    Horfield   55

What are they good for?
    Prisoners of war   56

A FRACTIOUS CITY   57

'The populace are likely to collect together in mobs on the slightest occasion'
    Riots in the eighteenth century   57

When riots rocked Old Market
    Unemployment riots of 1932   60

A peaceful protest
    The Bristol Bus Boycot   63

FIRE SERVICE   65

Fire
    A constant threat   65

MAKING MONEY 69

Shipshape and Bristol Fashion
    The port of Bristol in the Middle Ages 69
    Expanding the port 70
    Blankets and wine 71
    William Canygnes the Younger 72

A place to buy and sell
    Markets 75

The secular highlight of the year
    Fairs 80

All the fun of the fair
    - Charles Heal and Sons 82

What's in a name?
    Six brands named after the city 84
    Bristol Cars 85
    Bristol Brabazon 86
    Bristol Cream 88
    Bristol Cigarettes 89
    Bristol Lodekka Bus 91
    Bristol Blue Glass 91

BURDEN OF SHAME 93

Ill-gotten gains
    The Triangular Trade 93
    American Consulate 97

BRISTOL'S SWANSONG 99

An inadequate and old fashioned harbour
    Building the Floating Harbour 99

JOLLY COLLIERS 103

A once important industry
    Coal 103

SEIZED BY A SUDDEN DEATH 109

There died in a manner the whole strength of the town
    Plague 109

A treatment for 'hot livers, feeble brains and red pimply faces'
    The Hotwell 111

Laughter is the best medicine
    A cure for consumption? 112

PUBLIC HEALTH 115

'...the filth and stench were almost intolerable'
    Privys, cess pits and sewers 115

The sweetest and most wholesome waters
    Water supply 120

The third unhealthiest city in England
    Parks and open spaces 123
    Edgelands 127

The Downs
    'The people's park' 128

Scarlet Lychnis
    Bristol's Flower 130

HOSPITALS 131

From the cradle to the grave
    Bristol's hospitals 131

`Matron finds it necessary for her health to use a little porter'
    Bristol General Hospital 133

'There is something to be learned about mental disease each day'
    Psychiatric care 136

Britain's first woman doctor
    Elizabeth Blackwell 139

WHAT TO DO WITH THE DEAD? 141

'Strewn with bones'
    Graveyards and Cemeteries 141
    Some graveyards 142
    Bodies for science 146

SOURCES 149

ACKNOWLEDGEMENTS 151

INDEX 153

A word about the maze motif. This is from a roof boss in St Mary Redcliffe. It really does work as a maze. Though it does your head in if you follow it standing in the aisle, 10 metres below. A brick maze based on this design was built in Victoria Park in 1984, on the route of the twelfth century Redcliffe water pipe.

INTRODUCTION

Manson's *Bristol Miscellany* is my search for the soul of the city. I like to get to know the place I live in, to understand what makes it tick. As I wander round Bristol I find myself looking for the footprints of previous times. Why does our city look like it does? I want to understand why that building stands over there, why that road bends in that particular spot. I've lived in Bristol for over 45 years and I'm still finding new corners, new streets, new communities even.

There are few rules. To be honest, it's whatever grabs my interest. And I hope it will interest you. The geographical boundaries are pretty flexible as well. So *Manson's Bristol Miscellany* is exactly that. It's a personal history of Bristol and in no way is it definitive.

The *Bristol Miscellany* began life as a compendium of random facts. I began by focusing on lesser known stories. I became engrossed in hidden rivers, medieval walls, markets and fairs, prisons, the shameful slave trade, the treatment of mental illness, social housing, support for the poor, extreme weather. The list goes on.

It's been a long time in the making. I started 15 years ago, writing articles for the now sadly defunct *Bristol Review of Books* and it's grown from there. The 2020 Covid-19 lockdown gave me the opportunity to concentrate my energy and pull the strands together.

As the project grew the question was how to organise this cornucopia of information. The obvious answer was to arrange alphabetically. But then the connections get lost or obscured. The same with a chronological arrangement. In the end, I grouped topics under broad thematic headings. However, the book is still a miscellany rather than a comprehensive history,

Recently, there has been a resurgence of interest in Bristol's past. The city's story is being re-assessed and revised. After a conversation that had been going nowhere for decades, Edward Colston's Victorian statue was torn down and thrown in the docks. History lives and continues to evolve.

I'd be delighted if the *Miscellany* helps readers to see their environment just that little bit more clearly and, maybe, even embark on their own voyage of discovery. The aim is to rescue the past to give order to the present. As the Czech writer Ivan Klima (b.1931) wrote: 'To know a city is to love a city'. And to love a city hopefully means we will respect it and look after it. Bristol is a very special place. Let's keep it that way.'

Michael Manson

IN THE BEGINNING

A FEW MODEST MOUNDS

- Bristol's hill forts -

Bristol, admittedly, has no epic ancient monuments such as Maiden Castle or Silbury Hill. If you look carefully, however, there are a few modest mounds and unassuming hill-forts that point to settlement in prehistoric times.

One of the earliest remains is a Bronze Age (1800-600 BCE) barrow in Milltut Field, Badock's Wood, Southmead. It was excavated in 1873; a human skull was found in the centre of the mound, but little else.[1] The spot is marked by a stainless steel artwork that was installed in 2003 by the sculptor Michael Fairfax. The evocative prose on the obelisk was written by the sculptor's father, the poet and founder of the Arvon Foundation, John Fairfax (1930-2008). It reads:

'At Badock's wood ghostly windmill sails turn and like a rewound film spin through history to remote times when this was a burial place for a bronze age warrior. In that past landscape wolves prowled and nervy deer grazed while wild hog rooted among trees.'

Elsewhere, there are the remains of a

Bronze Age (1800-600 B.C.E.) barrow in Milltut Field, Badock's Wood, Southmead.

megalithic long barrow, now a garden rockery, in a private front garden on Druid Hill, Stoke Bishop.[2]

There are at least six Iron Age (600 BCE to AD 43) forts in the immediate vicinity of Bristol. They are all on top of hills and offer panoramic views. Though, maybe, fort is too strong a word as some were little more than cattle enclosures protected by a ditch. The most noticeable, and most clearly seen, is the 4.5 acre camp on which the Clifton Observatory

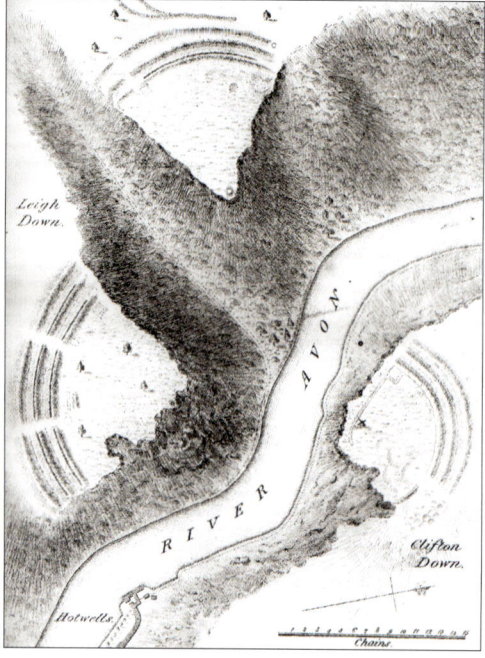

Three hill-forts cling to the Avon Gorge.

were established to guard such a strategic river crossing.[3]

Further north of the city three hill-forts stood on King's Weston Hill, a ridge with some precipitous drops, overlooking the wooded Hazel Brook Valley.[4] The largest of these was on the Blaise Castle Estate, which now has an eighteenth century gothic folly tower in the centre of its enclosure. Also, on King's Weston Hill, there were at least two small Iron Age round barrows.

Finally, it has long been speculated that the clump of trees, known as the Seven Sisters (though only three trees remain at the time of writing), on a tump on Durdham Downs, is a burial mound. Unfortunately, there is no archaeological evidence to confirm this thesis.

stands. The earthworks, originally two ditches, on the sides not protected by the sheer drop of the gorge, are best viewed if you approach along the footpath from Clifton Down Road.

Across the Avon Gorge were another two camps. To the south was Bower Walls, later known as Burgh Walls (8 acres). Now barely visible, the ramparts were levelled when the Victorian Burwalls House (c.1880) was built. To the north of this, overlooking Nightingale Valley, and also hard to discern because of ancient woodland, was another camp, Stokeleigh (7.5 acres). A prehistoric track once ran down Nightingale Valley to a ford across the Avon. In those days, at low water, during spring tides, the river could be crossed on foot on a reef of rocks. 'Boys are wet scarcely above the knees', wrote the historian, Samuel Seyer. It is suggested that these three camps

Prehistoric play equipment?

Below the Clifton Observatory is a short stretch of sloping rock that has been shined by the bottoms of many generations. One wonders for how long Bristol's children have skidded down this stone slide. Since time immemorial? Who knows? It is tempting to imagine that, perhaps, the Iron Age children who lived in the nearby hill-fort also partook of this pleasure?

IN THE BEGINNING

WHAT DID THE ROMANS DO FOR BRISTOL?
- Abonae -

Quite frankly, not much. The name Bristol didn't exist. What was later to become Bristol was somewhere Romans mostly passed by on their way to somewhere else. It would seem that the Romans were wary of our area's steep wooded hills, fast-running river and terrifying gorge, preferring to restrict their travel to the surrounding plateau. It has been suggested that the Saxon footprint of Bristol sits on the plan of an earlier Roman fortified town[5] but, at the present time, this is still conjecture.

Even so, the local landscape wasn't entirely empty. Adventurous Romano-British settlers established a number of extensive farms and villas in the area. Excavations have shown that the Iron Age hill-forts were utilised by the Romans. Blaise Castle hill-fort almost certainly contained a late Romano-British temple,[6] while a villa was built in the Clifton camp. When the foundations for the Blaise Castle folly were being dug in 1766 a large number of Roman coins were found.[7]

A Roman road, the grandly named Via Julia, ran from Aqua Sulis (Bath), to Abonae (Sea Mills). The road's exact route through Bristol has been lost, though traces are to be found on the Downs. In the low slanting light of a midwinter afternoon the ghostly shadow of the road is faintly visible. From the Downs the road then disappears under the gardens of Stoke Bishop, emerging as Mariners Drive and then Roman Way, not long after terminating at Sea Mills.

It was from the small, muddy port of Abonae that travellers set sail across the

The small, muddy port of Abonae.

In the low slanting light the ghostly shadow of the Via Julia is faintly visible.

Severn to the important Roman garrison town of Isca Silurum (Caerleon) on the river Usk in South Wales.

Kingsweston Villa was discovered in the 1940s during the construction of the Lawrence Weston housing estate. Excavations uncovered traces of a large stone farmstead with mosaics, under-floor heating and plunge pools. Coins indicate that it was last inhabited at the end of the third century.

Remains from the Brislington Villa – a small mosaic, pewter pots and roof tiles –

A small Roman villa workshop can be seen by the Portway at Sea Mills.

are held by Bristol Museum and Art Gallery. Excavations in 1899 revealed that the residents of the villa met a gruesome end. They were slaughtered in their own dining room and their bodies dumped in a well.[8] The building was then burnt down. By whom nobody knows – it was evidence of dangerous and lawless times.

In 2016, while land was being prepared for a residential site in Lockleaze, developers made an exciting and unexpected discovery – an extensive Romano-British farm overlooking Ashley Vale.[9] Once the soil had been stripped from the site a complete villa, with walled courtyard, outbuildings and wells along with a stone track-way, was revealed. The site had been in use for several hundred years, but was abandoned in the latter half of the fourth century AD.

Less impressive are the remains of what is claimed to be a small villa workshop, constructed AD 200, that can be seen by the Portway at Sea Mills.

Small finds from the Roman period continue to be unearthed. In 1954 a Roman rubbish tip was found in Southwood Drive, Combe Dingle. Excavations of Inns Court Farm, Knowle West, in 1996, found evidence of three Roman stone buildings from the third or fourth century that probably belonged to a nearby farming settlement.

Indications of Roman settlement have also been found in Upper Maudlin Street and in Bedminster Down (Brunel Road).

One gets the feeling that there is more of Bristol's Roman history to be discovered.

The key to Kingsweston Villa can be obtained from Blaise Castle Museum – a deposit of £10.00 is required.

In 2016, while land was being prepared for a residential site in Lockleaze, developers made an unexpected discovery – an extensive Romano-British farm overlooking Ashley Vale.
Photo: Sunbelt Survey.

A FLOURISHING COMMUNITY

- The Domesday Book -

In AD 410, the Romans pulled their garrisons out of Britain. Rome was under attack and the empire was falling apart. After 360 years of Roman rule Britannia went back to basics.

It would be another 600 years before Bristol was to become a settlement of any note. Bristol carries its history in its name: Brycg (bridge) Stow (place) is of Anglo-Saxon origin. *Bristol*, or a variant of it, makes it first appearance in the Anglo-Saxon records of the eleventh century – within a hundred years of its foundation.[10]

Coins were minted in Bristol during the reigns of Aethelred the Unready (968-1016) and Cnut (1016-35). Having a mint is a sure indication of the existence of a flourishing community.[11] However, Bristol, like London and Winchester, didn't get its own entry in the Domesday Book (1086). The Domesday Book focused on the countryside and rural possessions – the commissioners were instructed to find out how much cultivated land there was, what it was worth and who owned it.

Outlying areas did get a mention. Knowle was entered as a manor in its own right – with five villagers and six smallholders who appeared to share two ploughs. There were meadows, pastures and woodlands. The Domesday commissioners valued the land at 40 shillings.[12] The Manor of Clifton had a population of 30, half of whom were labourers. Bedminster had 25 villagers, 22 smallholders, a mill (Treen Mill, now the site of the Bathurst Basin), a priest and three slaves.[13]

Sixty years later, in the 1140s, Bristol was described as 'almost the richest of all towns in the kingdom'.[14] Bristol ranked in importance, after London, alongside Lincoln, Norwich and York. This was a rapid development, indeed.

WATER POWER

- Access to Important Trading Routes -

Bristol's early success as a trading centre, when it was safer and quicker to send goods by river rather than by unpredictable road, rested on its geographical position, Bristol had access to three important trading routes: the Avon, the Severn and the Wye. The Severn – the longest river in the United Kingdom – not only provided a gateway to Ireland and the Atlantic, but by travelling upstream it also offered a route to the heartland of England. The Severn curves in a great loop through five counties linking important trading centres such as the cathedral cities of Gloucester and Worcester, the abbey town of Tewkesbury, and even distant Shrewsbury.

On a smaller, more local scale, the Wye, once navigable beyond Monmouth, allowed trade with the borderlands of England and Wales. The famous half-timbered *Llandoger Trow* pub, an easy shout from Welsh Back, was named after the flat-bottomed boats, *trows*, that plied the Wye.

Bristol's other river, the Frome, while little used for navigation was nevertheless strategically important. It provided a moat for Bristol's Norman Castle and, until it was diverted, enclosed the early medieval city in a defensive loop.

Bristol's streams and brooks were also a source of water power. These days it's hard to imagine these gentle rivulets were once noisy

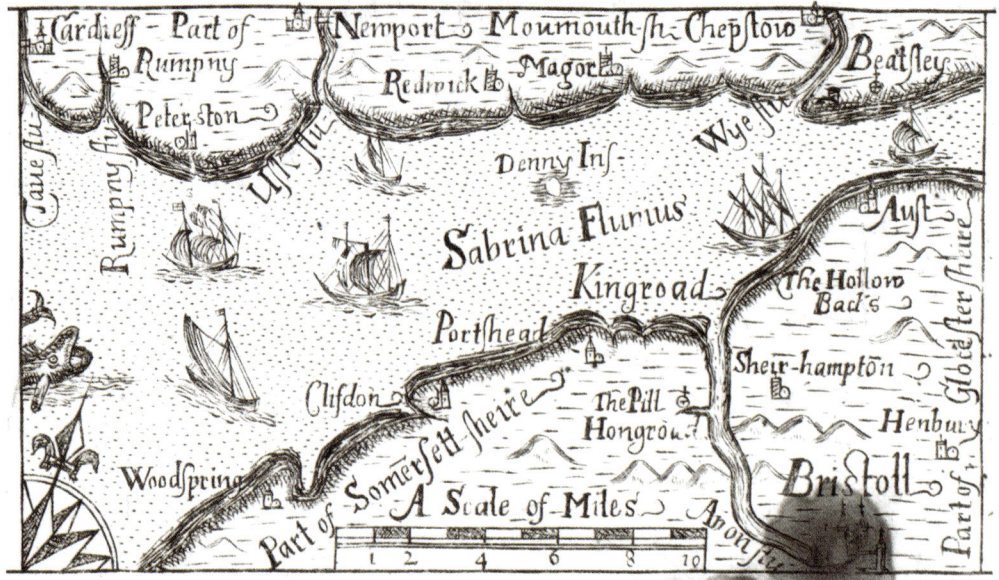

The Severn – the longest river in the United Kingdom – provided a gateway to Ireland and the Atlantic. Detail from Millerd's map 1673. © Bristol Culture (Bristol Museum & Art Gallery).

IN THE BEGINNING

The famous King Street pub, the *Llandoger Trow*, was named after the flat-bottomed boats, trows, that plied the Wye and the Severn.

Sailing the Avon with its twists, turns and gorge was a tricky business.

with industry. Many were dammed to form large ponds with water channelled through leats to turn water wheels. Mill ponds and the remains of industrial buildings can clearly be identified along the Frome, Hazel Brook, the Trym, and many other streams. Once, the sloosh of water wheels and the reverberation of grinding millstones filled the air of these now hushed valleys.

Bristol's landscape has been largely shaped by its watercourses. Even today the city is neatly divided north and south by the Cut and the docks. Many of Bristol's traffic problems are exacerbated by this watery divide.

- *Bristol's Rivers and Brooks* [15] -

The Avon and Frome, are fed by a surprisingly large number of streams – locally called brooks. Centuries of development means that many have been culverted or built over and are lost to view and forgotten – until damp rises up a wall, a cellar is unexpectedly flooded or pungent odours drift in the still air!

- **Ashton Brook** flows down Ashton Vale into the Avon.
- **Avon** rises near Tetbury and flows during its 78-mile meandering journey through Malmesbury, Chippenham, Bradford-on-Avon and Bath. Not to be confused with the Avon that runs through Stratford-upon-Avon. Indeed, there are five other Avons in England. Avon is Celtic for 'river' or 'water'; the Welsh equivalent being 'Afon'.
- **Beg Brook** is a tiny stream, approximately 400 metres long, that flows into the Frome, near Frenchay.
- **Brislington Brook** takes a long, slow and circuitous route through south-east Bristol. Initially two brooks – East and West – which both spring from the Dundry slopes. The brooks join together at Hengrove Park, trickle through Nightingale Valley and past St Anne's Wood before joining the Avon above Netham Lock.
- **Colliters Brook** also rises on the Dundry

The Avon and Frome, are fed by a surprisingly large number of streams. Horfield Brook, Mina Road Park.

slopes, runs by the Bristol City ground and is joined by Ashton Brook and Longmore Brook, entering the Avon at Ashton.
- **Coombe Brook** (also known as the Gossey) rises on Lodge Hill, East Bristol, flows through Royate Hill, is culverted under Greenbank Cemetery, emerges past the Black Swan pub, Stapleton Road, and joins the Frome under the M32.
- **Cranbrook** flows adjacent to Cranbrook Road, under the junction of Zetland Road and down to the present Montpelier Health Centre. From here it is known as Cutlers Mill Brook and is culverted. At the foot of Picton Street it flows eastwards to join Horfield Brook in Mina Road Park and thence to the Frome near the St Paul's roundabout of the M32.
- **Fishponds Brook** flows through Eastvillle Park and joins the Frome under the M32.
- **Frome** has its source in James Dyson's garden at Doddington and runs through Hambrook and Frenchay. In East Bristol it is also known as the Danny, though nobody knows why. These days the Frome enters the Floating Harbour under the Waterfall Steps in The Centre. It was diverted, in a remarkable feat of engineering, in 1247. Its original course ran along what is now St Stephen Street and Baldwin Street entering the Avon just by Bristol Bridge. Historically, the water quality of the Frome has been poor; more open drain than stream. However, over the last 20 years measures have been taken to cut pollution and there have been striking improvements. The recent presence of brown trout is an indicator of cleaner water quality, as is the occasional sighting of otter spraint and claw marks on the muddy river bank.

- **Hazel Brook** colloquially known as the Hen, rises north of what was once Filton Airfield, where it is supplemented by overflow water from the Cribbs Causeway Retail Park. It flows through Blaise Castle estate below lofty, wooded cliffs joining the Trym at Coombe Dingle. Dark mossy ponds and the carcasses of occasional ruined buildings mark the spot of long-defunct watermills.
- **Henry Sleed Stream**. This enigmatically named short brook runs through Oldbury Court Estate where it has been dammed to form two ponds and then joins the Frome.
- **Horfield Brook**[16] runs along Ashley Vale. In the nineteenth century a leat ran from the bubbling brook at Boiling Wells to provide water for cress beds and a fishpond. After disappearing under a railway embankment the brook makes a brief appearance in St Werburgh's before being furtively joined by Cutlers Mill Brook in Mina Road Park.
- **Horfield Brook** (number two!) runs between the Gloucester Road and North Road, St Andrew's. The brook is culverted and hardly in evidence. It joins the Cranbrook below the Zetland Road traffic lights.
- **Longmoor** is another of the Ashton Vale

IN THE BEGINNING

The Wain Brook flowing into and forming the lake in St Georges Park.

streams. It enters the Avon under the Cumberland Basin flyover.

- **Malago** rises from the Dundry slopes and flows north into the Avon. At one stage it must have been faster flowing than now. It is said that the stretch below Bishport Avenue was once navigable and used for the transport of stone from Dundry Hill.
- **Pigeonhouse Stream** rises on the Dundry slopes and feeds into the Malago.
- **Trym** rises in Southmead, flowing through Badock Woods, Westbury on Trym and Coombe Dingle before entering the Avon at Sea Mills. The muddy Sea Mills creek was the site of the tiny Roman port of Abonae.
- **Wain Brook** flows through St George's Park, feeding the man-made pleasure lake.

There are also a number of seasonal streams, or winterbournes, such as on the Dundry Northern Slopes and Arnos Vale Park, that appear only when the water table is high.

Moonlight on the Malago

Fredal, Brendal and Barbaral
Used to make I heave a sigh.
Monical and Sweet Veronical
Each the one I thought for I.
Until I met our Glorial
From Beminster and ther'e no doubt
When its moonlight on the Malago
Glorial an I goes out.

Adge Cutler (1930-74)

ENDNOTES

1. Ginsell, L.V., *Prehistoric Bristol*. Bristol Branch of the Historical Association, 1969, p.10.
2. ibid., p.7.
3. Tratman, E.E., *The Prehistoric Archaeology of the Bristol Region* in *Bristol and Its Adjoining Counties*, 1955, Bristol, p 160.
4. Lock, G. and Relston, I.. *Atlas of Hillforts of Britain and Ireland* [On Line]. https://hillforts.arch.ox.ac.uk/
5. Nicholls, J.F. & Taylor,J., *Bristol Past and Present*, 1881, Arrowsmith, Vol.1, p.27.
6. Fowler, P.J., *Hill-Forts, A.D. 400-700*, in ed. Jesson, M. and Hill, D. *The Iron Age and its Hill-Forts*, 1971, University of Southampton, p.208.
7. Evans,J., *A Chronological Outline of the History of Bristol*, 1824, Bristol, p. xxix.
8. Branigan.K., *The Romans in the Bristol Area*, 1969, Bristol Branch of the Historical Association, p.8.
9. https://cotswoldarchaeology.co.uk/excavation-of-a-roman-villa-complex-in-lockleaze/ Accessed 9/12/2019.
10. Walker, D., *Bristol in the Early Middle Ages*, 1971, Bristol Branch of the Historical Association, p.4.
11. ibid., p.5.
12. Morris, J., *Domesday Book - Somerset*, 1980, Phillimore, 98a.
13. ibid.,86c.
14. Sherborne, J., *The Port of Bristol in the Middle Ages*, 1971, Bristol Branch of the Historical Association, p.3.
15. Bristol Avon River Authority – map, untitled, pre-1974.
16. The Big Blue Map of Bristol, Crown Copyright: Bristol City Council 100023406

POWER AND POLITICS

COUNTY LIMITS

- The County of Bristol -

The County of Bristol was created by Edward III (1312-77) in 1373.

Prior to this Bristol comprised two distinct and separate settlements: Bristol to the north of the River Avon and the parishes of Redcliffe, St Thomas and Temple to the south.

To complicate matters even more, Temple was administered by the Knights Templar, the fighting monastic order that guarded the route to Jerusalem during the crusades. The name lives on, through Temple Church and Temple Meads though 'Temple Quarter' is a twenty-first century marketing concoction. The Knights Templar, with their peculiar round chapel modelled on the Church of the Holy Sepulchre in Jerusalem, had their own market, courts and answered only to the Pope. Needless to say they were unpopular with the Kings of England and were a niggling annoyance to their neighbours.

In 1247, a royal charter attempted to bring together the communities north and south of the Avon. With the old wooden bridge being replaced by a new stone structure it was hoped

Temple Church. The Knights Templar had their own church, market and courts and answered only to the Pope.

that the two communities would become unified. 'This year the Bridge of Bristol began to be founded, and the inhabitants of Redcliffe, Temple and Thomas were incorporated and combined with the town of Bristol.'[1]

Yet the royal decree was embraced only half-heartedly. Redcliffe continued to collect its own taxes, hold its own courts and use its own gallows. This caused frequent antagonism. The residents on either side of the river were not averse to a sporadic raiding party. On one occasion a horde of Bristolians, headed by the Mayor, swarmed over the bridge to rescue a man and who had been incarcerated in a Redcliffe gaol. At the same time they also plundered 500 marks worth of property.[2] It was to be another 126 years before the communities north and south of the river became finally and fully united.

In 1373, Bristol was the first town outside London to be granted county status. This new arrangement meant that Bristol could raise its own taxes and its citizens came under the jurisdiction of its own local court.[3] Prior to this, the inhabitants had to travel, depending on which side of the Avon they lived, to the county courts of either Gloucestershire or Somerset.

Bristol Castle, sitting at the centre of the newly established city, was not included in the county boundaries and remained marooned as a part of Gloucestershire until 1629.

The Temple area also remained outside this agreement. As late as 1532 the Corporation

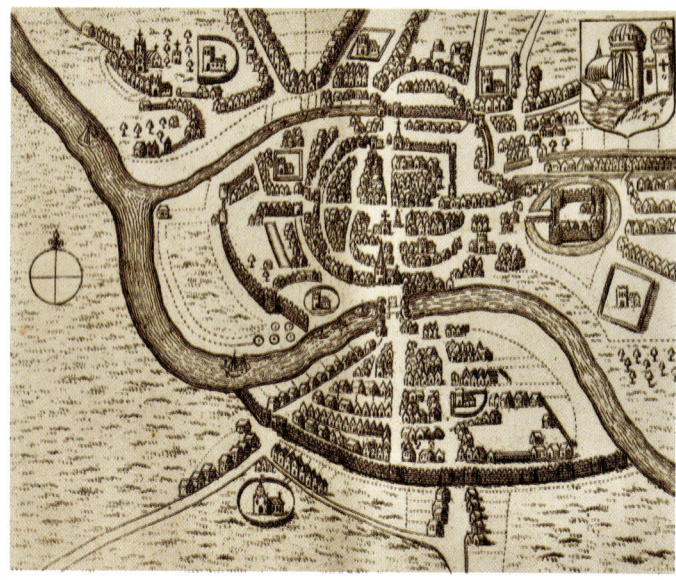

Prior to 1373 Bristol comprised two distinct and separate settlements. Bristol to the north of the Avon and the parishes of Redcliffe, Temple and St Thomas to the south.

of Bristol claimed that Temple was an unruly area and a refuge for outlaws. Temple's independence came to an abrupt end in 1543 with the suppression of the monasteries by Henry VIII (1509-47).[4]

The enhanced county status cost Bristol 600 gold marks (a mark was six shillings and eight pence – 1/3rd of a pound).

The new county of Bristol included the channel of the Avon out to the Severn, and from there to the rocky islands of Steep Holm and Flat Holm in the Bristol Channel.[5] Thus giving protection for ships entering the port.

Apart from some small adjustments in 1777, Bristol's boundaries remained virtually unchanged until 1835. The boundaries were extended again in 1897 and 1904 by the Bristol Extension Acts. In 1935 Lawrence Weston and Brentry came under the auspices of Bristol, while in 1951 the planned new suburbs of Stockwood, Hartcliffe and Withywood were included.[6]

POWER AND POLITICS

EASING THE WAY TO HEAVEN
- Church and Chapel -

Religion permeated every aspect of medieval life. At the time of the Reformation in the 1530s no less than 18 parish churches were crowded in and around the central area of the town[7] – quite a number for a population of about 10,000.

Beyond the walls the town was ringed by a range of ecclesiastical establishments. There was an abbey, a priory, houses of friars, and a number of hospitals. They were all pretty low grade – nothing like the abbeys of Glastonbury, Tintern or Gloucester. But they did have a constant presence, and at least they could feed the poor and in some cases look after the dying. The hospitals were more like today's hospices. Little could be done to cure illness, but at least the religious atmosphere could ease the way to heaven.

The money to support these establishments came from tithes and donations. While today's super-rich buy mega-yachts, their medieval equivalents would fund church building, almshouses and chantries.

Relationships between Bristol and the surrounding ecclesiastical houses were not always good. Friction was caused by the affirmation of certain ecclesiastical privileges such as sanctuary and the assertion that they did not fall within the jurisdiction of Bristol.

Beyond the walls Bristol was ringed by a range of ecclesiastical establishments.

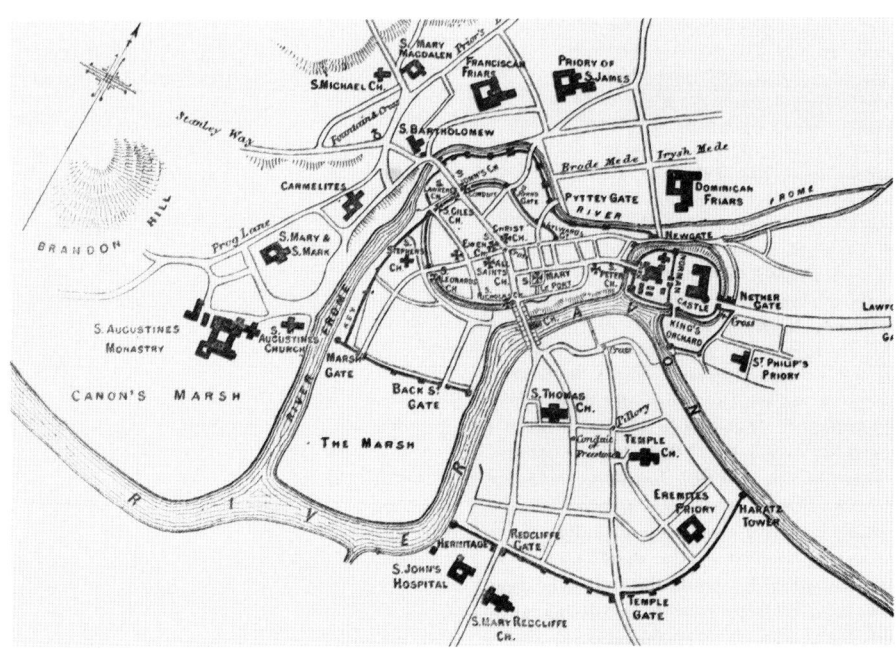

ST ANNE'S HOLY WELL

- Bristol's Holy Well -

It seems remarkable than soon after Henry VII (1485-1509) claimed the crown at the Battle of Bosworth Field in 1485 he made a pilgrimage to Bristol.[8]

The King came to St Anne's Wood, in the manor of Brislington, to drink the waters of a holy well. Although the well is now little more than a fenced-off circle of stones on a slope between St Anne's Wood and Nightingale Valley, this humble watering place was once a focus of pilgrimage. (There are two Nightingale Valleys in the Bristol region – this is in south east Bristol; the other is across the Clifton Suspension Bridge in Leigh Woods.)

The fourteenth century antiquarian William of Worcester mentioned the well in his description of Bristol and writes that it formed part of a small chapel cared for by the monks of Keynsham Abbey.

The well has a history of neglect and is lucky to have survived. In 1922 the well was reported to be blocked with rubbish and overgrown with weeds. Fortunately, the Corporation shortly afterwards acquired this interesting historical relic and the surrounding woodland.[9] Two years later a canopy of 'traditional Somerset design' was erected over the restored sacred spring giving it the unfortunate appearance of a gnome's wishing well.

St Anne is the patron saint of sailors, ports and harbours. Quite why this spot, a couple of miles from the medieval docks of Bristol, was venerated is not known. Perhaps some small miracle was once performed here?

Soon after Henry VII claimed the crown at the Battle of Bosworth Field in 1485 he made a pilgrimage to St Anne's Well.

The City and County of Bristol
Bristol became a cathedral city in 1542 when the Diocese of Bristol was established.[10] Henry VIII dissolved the monastery of St Augustine and then re-designated the abbey as a cathedral church for the new Bristol Diocese.

How do we know?
Much of the information we have about early Bristol and its governance comes from *The Little Red Book* (1344-1574) and *The Great Red Book* (1380-1546). These are minute books that contain resolutions and bye-laws. These intriguing ancient books still exist and are held by Bristol Archives.

POWER AND POLITICS

ISLANDS IN THE BRISTOL CHANNEL
- Steep Holm and Flat Holm -

Under the charter of 1373, these two strategically important limestone holms (holm is Norse for island) marked the limit of Bristol's jurisdiction.

Somerset had the southern corner of Steep Holm, Gloucestershire the northern corner and Bristol the eastern corner.[11] Though nobody seems to have taken too much notice of these divisions. More important was the control of shipping in the Severn Estuary leading up to the mouth of the Avon.

Steep Holm lies five miles west of Weston-super-Mare, while Flat Holm is a couple of miles further north. Geologically these two precipitous islands are an extension of the limestone Mendips.

Nobody lives permanently on the holms now, though it is possible to take a day trip.

The landscape is littered with relics that hint at an interesting and varied past. On Steep Holm there are the remains of an Augustinian priory, a ruined farm house, barracks, gun emplacements, military batteries and a searchlight post. The writer, John Fowles (1926-2005), wrote of Steep Holm 'the

In 1373 the county boundary was extended into the Severn Estuary. Denny Island, the northernmost extent of Bristol's jurisdiction, is on the horizon.

atmosphere of the island contrives, because of all the old military paraphernalia to be both very beautiful and very bizarre...'[12]

Flat Holm, on the Welsh side of the channel, plays a significant role in the history of telecommunications. It was from here, in 1897, that the immortal words 'Are you ready?' were tapped in Morse code to the 21-year-old Italian inventor Guglielmo Marconi (1874-1937), who was three-and-a-half miles away at Lavernock Point in South Wales.[13] This was the world's first radio transmission across a stretch of water.

Today, both the 'holms' are nature reserves. The 50 acre, uninhabited, Steep Holm is owned by the Kenneth Allsop Memorial Trust. Since 1996 Steep Holm has been under the administration of North Somerset Council. Flat Holm has been quietly annexed by Wales and is now overseen by the Cardiff Harbour Authority.

A MEETING PLACE AT TIMES OF STRESS OR CELEBRATION

- Bristol's High Cross -

The High Cross was built at the focal point of the city – the intersection of the four main streets.

Town or high crosses were familiar features of historic town landscapes. Apart from their obvious religious significance they served as a central point for the community: a meeting place at times of stress and celebration. It was from the cross that the town crier would read royal proclamations, announce elections and give news of victories or invasions. It was also a good spot for itinerant traders to set up their unofficial stalls.

It is a surprising fact that Bristol's High Cross currently stands not in Bristol but 36 miles away in Stourhead Park, Wiltshire.

The first mention of a cross in Bristol was in 1247. It is uncertain where it stood at that time. In 1373, to commemorate Bristol's new status as a city and county, the High Cross was built at the focal point of the city – the intersection of the four main streets.[14] It was an impressive multi-tiered structure, as tall as the surrounding buildings, with niches for statues of kings and saints. Bristol's slender and elegant cross was a source of great civic pride. If royalty visited, it would be cleaned and spruced up. When Henry VII stopped by in 1490 it was repainted and gilded, likewise when Elizabeth I (1558-1603) was entertained in the city in 1574.

By 1733, the cross was not only a hindrance to traffic but also unsafe. A silversmith who lived opposite the cross said that 'in every high wind his house and life were endangered by its shaking and threatening to fall'.[15] The cross was consequently dismantled and placed out of the way on College Green. But it didn't stay there for long. In 1768, the cross was 'disposed of in a most illegitimate manner'[16] and transported to Stourhead Park. This is where this city centre icon remains today, startlingly out of place, overlooking the park's gorgeous Arcadian landscape.

That's not the end of the story. In 1851 – the time of the Great Exhibition when an appreciation of everything gothic was sweeping the land – a scaled down replica cross was built and placed, yet again, on

POWER AND POLITICS

College Green. And yet again, it was soon on the move. The facsimile cross was shifted to a supposedly more central position, opposite the cathedral, when a marble statue of Queen Victoria was erected in its place.

This is where it stood until 1950, when E. Vincent Harris, the architect of the new Council House, demanded the cross's removal as, he declared, it spoilt the view of his splendid new, unicorn topped, building.

A few pieces of the dismal 1851 reproduction were salvaged and in 1956 a stunted version of the cross was erected in a shady corner of Berkeley Square.

There have been a number of attempts to retrieve Bristol's original High Cross from its bucolic surroundings and return it to its rightful place. Corn Street is now pedestrianised and traffic is discouraged from entering Broad Street. So there is space for the Cross to be

(Left) Bristol's elegant High Cross, startlingly out of place, overlooks Stourhead's gorgeous Arcadian landscape. (Right) In 1956, a stunted version of the replica cross was erected in a shady corner of Berkeley Square.

re-established. Looking to the future, 2033 will be the tercentenary of the cross's removal: a fitting date for its return. Let the negotiations begin...

- Other Bristol Crosses -

There were other, smaller crosses scattered around Bristol.
- **Bewell's Cross**. Also called Gallows Cross, this lost cross stood at the top of St Michael's Hill on the road to Wales. The cross also served as a boundary marker for the city.
- **Don John's Cross**. This was originally placed at the road divide to Kingswood and Hanham. Its origins are vague – some fancifully think it commemorates a long forgotten Spanish nobleman, others that it was a marker for the Kingswood forest boundary. The ignominious plinth of this cross is to be seen outside St George Library, where it was placed in 2000.

- **Stallage Cross**. In Temple Street, a market cross was erected when Temple Fee was under the control of the Knights Templar.
- **Old Market Cross**. At the west end of Old Market Street (now the underpass). Mentioned in 1470 by the antiquarian William of Worcester.
- **St Peter's Cross**. Erected over the well of St Edith, by St Peter's Church, in the mid-fifteenth century.[17]
- **The Red Cross**. Redcross Street. Presumably made of local red sandstone, it was situated at the west end of Redcross Street. Its origins and date are lost in the fog of time.

A CASTLE, A SHIP, AN EEL AND A FISH
- Bristol's Coat of Arms -

Bristol's coat of arms was officially granted in 1569, though a seal featuring a castle and a ship, accompanied by fish and a large eel, first appeared in the reign of Edward 1 (1272-1307).[18] The ship is not, as some believe, Cabot's *Matthew* which would have sailed nearly 180 years later.

The coat of arms has been modified over the years. The motto 'Virtue et Industria' (by Virtue and Industry) probably appeared in the eighteenth century.

Bristol Coat of Arms 1975.

Bristol Mayoralty seals 1428-1463.

POWER AND POLITICS

WHERE'S THE CASTLE?
- Bristol Castle -

Bristol's coat of arms shows a ship and a castle. Ships, though not commercially used, are still in evidence in Bristol's docks. But where is the castle?

These days it is hard to believe that after the White Tower in the Tower of London, Bristol Castle had the largest Norman keep – five storeys high with towers on its corners – in the country. At the time it was built it was one of the strongest and most impressive castles in England.

The Normans came to Bristol in 1068. Initially, they built a wooden motte-and-bailey on a hillock to the east of the original Anglo-Saxon settlement – what is now Castle Park.[19] It was bounded by the Frome to the north and the Avon to the south.

A more substantial stone castle was constructed on the same site around 1110 by Robert Earl of Gloucester (died 1147), an illegitimate son of Henry 1 (1100-35). For 500 years the castle's keep, towers and

Bristol Castle. At the time it was built it was one of the strongest and most impressive castles in the land.

Several houses in Old Market were constructed with salvaged masonry from the castle.

battlements were an impressive presence dominating the Bristol skyline and acting over the years as a prison, a royal residence and during the reign of Henry VIII (1509-47) a mint. In 1141, King Stephen (1135-54) was incarcerated here during the civil war with Matilda (1102-67), while the future Henry II (1154-89) spent some of his boyhood years in the castle.

When Bristol was granted county status in 1373, the castle was not included in the deal. The castle remained an island of Gloucestershire within the County of Bristol. It soon became a refuge for 'thieves, malefactors, or other disorderly livers' seeking sanctuary.[20]

Finally, to overcome this problem, in 1629, the castle came under the jurisdiction of Bristol.

Accommodation in the castle was basic. With time, its cold stone passages and unglazed windows meant it was not fit for a king. The chapel, the Royal Hall and Chamber all fell to ruin.

In 1446, Henry VI (1422-61) preferred lodgings offered by the Knights Hospitalers in Redcliffe Pit[21] while in 1474, Edward IIII (1461-83), who was on his way to France, stayed with the Abbot in St Augustine's.[22] As did the newly crowned Henry VII in 1486.[23] In 1534, the topographer, John Leland (1503-52), described the castle as 'tendith to ruine'.[24]

The castle was dismantled in 1654 by the command of Oliver Cromwell (1599-1658). An order was sent to every householder to assist in the demolition.[25] Remarkably, it was pulled down in the space of merely two weeks. The stones were swiftly scattered round the city and used in other building projects. It is said that several houses in Old Market were constructed with salvaged masonry.

Little remains of this once massive structure apart from a couple of cellars, a few mounds and the name Castle Park.

POWER AND POLITICS

THE WALLS CAME TUMBLING DOWN

- Walls and Gateways -

Like all self-respecting Norman towns Bristol not only had a castle but was also surrounded by walls. The gateways into Bristol were for protection as well as the collection of tolls and taxes on traders. As the town grew, where possible, the walls and gateways were rebuilt correspondingly. When the Frome was diverted in the 1230s, a new wall, Marsh Wall, was constructed along the north side of the present day King Street.

Portwall was the strongest. Built in the thirteenth century, it protected Redcliffe and Temple.[26] With just two gates, Redclifffe Gate and Temple Gate, the solid walls were further strengthened by eight bastions. (Today's Portwall Lane follows part of its route. In the 1990s, excavations uncovered a stretch of the wall that was subsequently preserved and can now be viewed through dusty reinforced glass along Rivergate, Temple Quarter.)

A yawning ditch along the Portwall's base also acted as a formidable barrier.[27] The then undeveloped St Mary Redcliffe remained outside the walls; to include this small church and the unpopulated Redcliffe Hill within the defences of the city would have been needlessly expensive and strategically unwise.

At Lawford's Gate, at the east end of Old Market Street, there was no defensive wall. Here, the perimeter of Bristol was fortified by The Great Ditch which ran in a curve from the Frome to the Avon.

It was to the north that Bristol was at its weakest. The possibility of being overlooked by potential assailants from the commanding heights of St Michael's Hill and Brandon Hill

In the 1730s, Temple Gate was replaced by a new gateway with passageways on either side for the safety of pedestrians.

made the town appear, and indeed feel, vulnerable.

In 1643, when Prince Rupert (1619-82) reclaimed Bristol during the Civil War (1642-51), the royalists found the Portwall impregnable. After half an hour 'bodies lay on the ground like rotten sheep'.[28] Meanwhile, a weak point (at the top of what is now Park Street) was soon identified and the three miles of recently dug defensive ditches and earthworks to the east, north and west of the city were quickly breached.[29]

During quieter times the problem with gateways was traffic congestion. In the 1730s, Redcliffe and Temple Gates were replaced by new gateways, both with passageways on either side for the safety of pedestrians.

The first gate to be removed for good was Back Gate, in 1738, to allow easier access to Queen Square.[30] Castle Gate was bought in

Broad Street with St John's gateway. By 1800, nearly all the gateways had gone.

1766 for salvage by William Reeve, owner of the Crews Hole Copper Works, and its statues of English kings placed in his gothic archway at Arnos Court.[31]

By the 1760s Bristol was bursting at the seams. The busiest gate was Lawford's. This was taken down in 1769 and not replaced. Surrounding the city with a wall was no longer practical. During the eighteenth century there had been a surge in population matched by a growth in buildings. At the end of Thomas Street an unofficial opening had been hacked through the once unassailable Portwall for easier access to the fields of Redcliffe Meads. Nobody built walls anymore; taxes had been abolished for goods coming through the gates way back in 1545. The city was looking to the future, looking outwards.

There were, however, still instances when the people craved the security of a wall. In 1715, the gates were ordered to be closed when there was the national threat of a Jacobite rebellion.[32] Indeed, several times during the eighteenth century the colliers from the King's Wood marched on the city in protest at price rises or turnpike tolls.[33] But on such occasions the closing of the creaking gates was more symbolic than practical.[34]

In reality, there was no money for the upkeep of gates and no real necessity. The prosperous were moving to the suburbs – many to the higher ground of Clifton. There was a new, wide bridge across the Avon and fashionable squares, built in fancy red brick and dressed with Bath stone. There was an aspiration for the Hotwell to become the new Bath. Ambitious plans were drawn up for the King's Down to the north, while in the east, beyond Lawrence and Barton Hill there were all manner of thriving, smelly, smoky, noisy enterprises. Walls and gates, who needed them? By 1800, nearly all the gateways had gone. Today, only St John's gateway – an integral part of St John's church – remains.

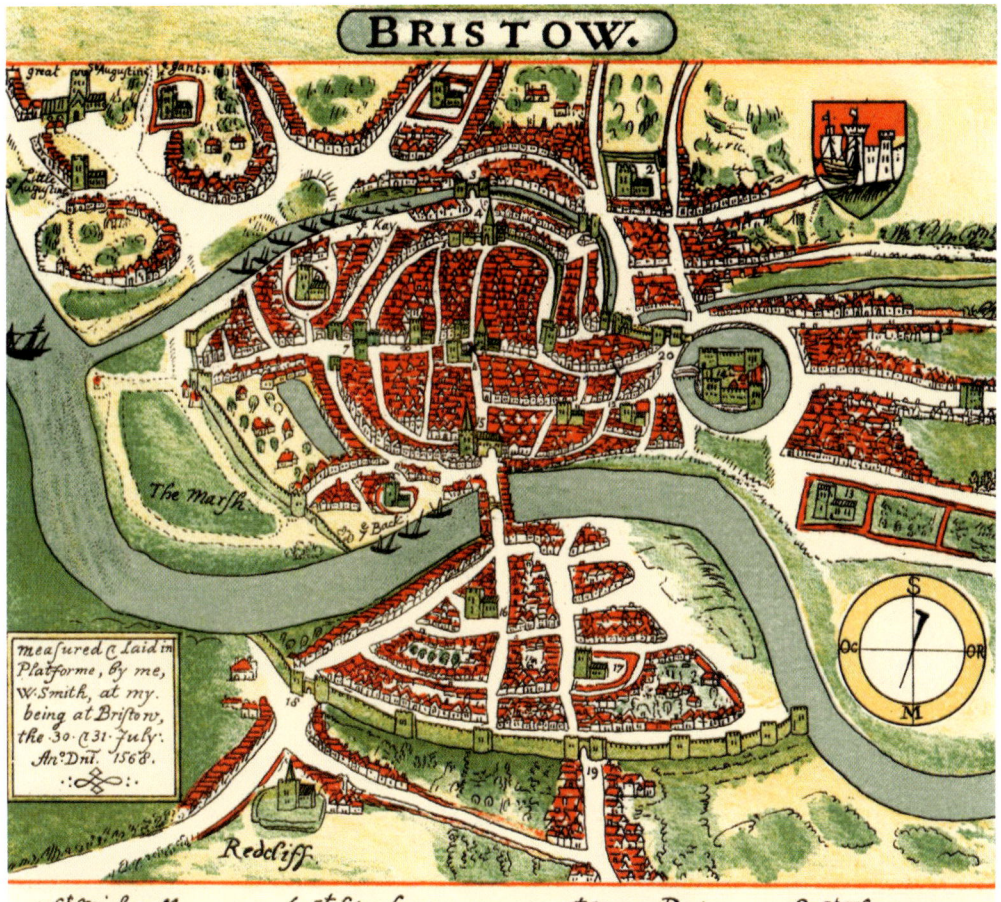

William Smith's map of Bristol, created following his visit in July 1568. Portwall was the strongest wall. Built in the thirteenth century, it protected Redcliffe and Temple. With just two gates, Redcliffe Gate and Temple Gate, the solid walls were further strengthened by bastions.

COINING IT

- The Mint -

Over the years, Bristol has had several mints. Indeed, the first evidence for the existence of Bristol comes from a few small silver pennies struck during the reign of Aethelred the Unready (968-1016).[35]

In 1272 it was recorded that there were 'twelve furnaces at York and twelve furnaces in Bristol for melting silver, and hammering and stamping perfect money.'[36] Initially, the mint was probably within the castle precinct though in 1422 a new mint was set up in Norton's Mansion (later St Peter's Hospital), opposite St Peter's Church.

Forging or tampering with coins was not to be recommended. In 1555, four men were drawn, hanged and quartered – with their remains displayed at the gates – for illegally coining money.[37] In 1695, a woman from Thomas Street was sentenced to be 'burnt in the street' for clipping coins.[38]

The last coins to be minted in Bristol were during the reign of William III (1689-1702). In 1696, there was a national 'Great Re-coinage' when old-style hand-hammered silver coins were replaced by new milled currency manufactured by a screw press. The milled edge of the coin was to deter fraudulent clipping. Branch mints were set up in Bristol, Chester, Exeter, Norwich and York.[39] Bristol's coins were recognisable by the letter 'B' under the head. The old coins were replaced by their weight value rather than their face value. 'Many people sustained considerable loss.'[40]

The Great Re-coinage was funded through a new tax, the window tax. The occupier of every house was to pay two shillings a year, with an additional payment of eight shillings for a house with over ten windows.[41] This unpopular 'tax on light', nicknamed 'daylight robbery', continued in various forms until 1851 when it was replaced by the House Tax.

The Mint (St Peter's Hospital – bombed 1940). The last coins to be struck in Bristol were during the reign of William III.

POWER AND POLITICS

'REALLY, VERY UGLY'
- The Mansion House -

The first official residence of the mayor, the Mansion House, was on the north east side of Queen Square. It was bought by the Corporation in 1783 – 25 years after London had built its own Mansion House. Compared with London's flamboyant classical building the Bristol Mansion House was a modest affair. Nevertheless, the Corporation was criticised for extravagant expenditure of public money on carpets, chandeliers and furniture.[42]

The spending spree continued with the purchase of a state coach for £622 and a new mayoral sword and chain.

The Mansion House was a focus for rioters in 1831 when it was attacked, looted and set on fire. The building was left as a smouldering shell. The Mayor's lodging was then moved to temporary accommodation in Great George Street.

Elmdale, the current Lord Mayor's Mansion House on Clifton Down, was presented to the city in 1874 by Alderman Thomas Proctor (1811-76), fertiliser magnate and Bristol benefactor. This large, but unpretentious Victorian house, faced with red sandstone excavated on the spot, was built by Proctor with the intention of leaving it to the city after his death. Proctor specified that the rooms should be spacious but not ostentatious. Outside, the house's muted, Italianate style was described by architectural historians Gomme and Jenner as 'really, very ugly'.[43] When the flag is flying and the sun is shining on the Bristol coat of arms it's not that bad!

Elmdale, the current Lord Mayor's Mansion House on Clifton Down, was presented to the city in 1874.

Mansion House in around 1975.

Spacious but not ostentatious. The Banquet Room inside the Mansion House, c.1975.

WHO ORDERED THE UNICORNS?

- City Hall -

City Hall. The foundation stone was laid in 1935. But the building wasn't officially opened until 1956.

The foundation stone for City Hall, then known as the Council House, was laid in 1935. The architect, E. Vincent Harris (1876-1971), had already built the County Hall in Taunton, a mini-version of what we see in Bristol. The shell of the building, a reinforced concrete frame, was almost complete when war was declared in 1939. During the Second World War (1939-45) the bare Council Chamber was used as a 'British Restaurant'; in reality a canteen for those bombed-out of their homes or not able to cook for themselves. Even after the war there were shortages and the building wasn't officially opened until 1956.

The Portland stone figure in the central archway, carved by Charles Wheeler (1892-1974), has variously been described as a generic Elizabethan seaman or more specifically John Cabot.[44] The wide Lutyen's inspired brick exterior is imposing but bland.

When the two gilded unicorns by David McFall (1919-88) arrived on site for installation nobody knew where to put them. It seems that Harris, who was on holiday in France at the time, had forgotten he'd ordered them and they weren't on the architectural plans.[45] But once installed the glowing unicorns add much needed pizzazz. Nevertheless, it is a building of confidence and pride. College Green, in

POWER AND POLITICS

Construction of City Hall with foundation work well underway in October 1936, and reinforced concrete frame nearing completion in March 1939.

City Hall. The Lord Mayor's parlour even had a fireplace. Albeit with a coal effect electric fire.

The two unicorns on the roof of City Hall add much needed pizzazz.

front of the building, provides a public space for crowds to gather at times of celebration and crisis. The shallow moat comes in useful for less peaceful occasions.

Inside, in spite of post-war austerity, the interior is rather splendid. The quality of workmanship by Bristol construction firm Cowlin & Son is superb. The walls and corridors of the entrance hall are lined with Doulting stone from the Mendips.[46] In the foyer a clock encircled by signs of the zodiac, with its own wind dial, references Bristol's maritime past. The names of the mayors of Bristol, dating back to 1216, are carved into the stone walls of the Council Chamber. Although the semi-abstract ceiling in the Conference Hall painted by W.T. Monnington (1902-76) has a Festival of Britain vibe, there is little reference to modernism in the remainder of the building. The Lord Mayor's parlour even had a fireplace, albeit with a coal-effect electric fire.[47]

In 2012, George Ferguson, Bristol's first directly elected mayor, on his first day in office, changed the name of the building to City Hall.[48]

Mayor
The first mayor of Bristol was appointed in 1216. Queen Victoria extended the title to Lord Mayor in 1899. The Lord Mayor is appointed annually; not to be confused with the elected Mayor of Bristol, or the Regional Mayor.

Members of Parliament
Since 1283 Bristol has returned two members to Parliament. In 1885 this number was increased to four.

POWER AND POLITICS

'WHAT SHADOWS WE ARE, AND WHAT SHADOWS WE PURSUE'

- Edmund Burke 1729-1797 -

Bristol's most famous Member of Parliament was the Irish-born statesman and orator Edmund Burke. He was MP for Bristol from 1774-80, though he hardly ever visited the city, preferring to remain at his home in Beaconsfield, Buckinghamshire.

Some Bristolians were alarmed to find out that not only had they elected an anti-slave trader as their MP but Burke was also a supporter of American Independence. The electorate should have paid more attention to his speeches. Burke's view was that he was elected for his own beliefs which were not necessarily the viewpoint of the electorate. 'He is not a member of Bristol, he is a member of parliament'.[49] This is a debate that continues today

Burke wisely decided not to stand for re-election. In his farewell speech he uttered the memorable metaphysical words 'What shadows we are, and what shadows we pursue.'[50]

Burke's statue in the Centre was unveiled in 1894 and paid for by tobacco manufacturer, Mr W.H. Wills.[51] The inscription on the front of the pedestal reads 'I wish to be a member of parliament to have my share of doing good and resisting evil'. Politicians please note.

A copy of this statue, but with a different inscription, stands in Washington DC.

The great Irish-born statesman and orator Edmund Burke was M.P. for Bristol from 1774-1780, though he hardly ever visited the city.

Edmund Burke as he appeared in Bell's Constitutional Classics 1814.

THE POWER BEHIND THE THRONE?

- Society of Merchant Venturers -

Who really was the power behind the throne? The Society of Merchant Venturers has played a significant, and sometimes shadowy, role in the history of Bristol's trade, commerce and governance. Indeed, there are times when it hasn't been clear who was running the city. Was it the City Council? Or was it the Society of Merchant Venturers?

The Society of Merchant Venturers was established under a Royal Charter in December 1551. Through this and subsequent Royal Charters, the Merchant Venturers gained control over most of the Bristol's imports and exports, collecting duty and taxes, for nearly 250 years.

In 1690, a committee was set up by the Society of Merchant Venturers to petition Parliament to end the Royal African Company's monopoly of the 'African trade'. But the Society didn't want to abolish the trade, it wanted to join in! Subsequently, eight years later Bristol's merchants became involved in the trafficking of enslaved Africans. Slave trading from Bristol reached a peak in 1732, surpassing London and accounting for almost half of the ships sailing to Africa.

The Merchant Venturers was an influential body. It had wide reaching powers but, unlike the Council, was not elected and publicaly accountable. In the eighteenth century membership of the Council and the Merchant Venturers appeared interchangeable.

In 1750, the African Company was set up by Act of Parliament and any merchant, whether or not a member of the Society,

Merchant's Hall on Clifton Down Road, a few doors away from the Mansion House.

could join on payment of a fee. The managing committee of nine representatives was shared between London, Liverpool and Bristol, with the Merchant Venturers collecting the local membership subscriptions. So not only were many of their members intimately involved with the hideous slave trade, the Society was also part of a national group responsible for overseeing the business.

In 1789, the Merchant Venturers opposed William Wilberforce's (1759-1833) proposed Act for the total abolition of the slave trade. Additionally, they made their hall available for meetings of anti-abolitionists such as the West India merchants, plantation owners and local manufacturers.

The tide was slowly turning. Bristol's Quakers (many of whom had profited from the slave trade and slave labour) resolved to boycott the slave trade. In Bristol, the abolitionists were led by Joseph Harford (1741-1815),[52] a Quaker banker and brass manufacturer. Harford became master of the Merchant Venturers in 1796.

Slave trading was eventually made illegal in 1807 and slavery itself was finally abolished in Great Britain and its colonies in 1833.

Today, the role of the Society of Merchant Venturers is different. According to their website:

'*The men and women of the Society of Merchant Venturers work with and support people and communities from the wider Bristol area. We do this through education, care for older people, charitable giving and social enterprise.*'[53]

The Society of Merchant Venturers's headquarters is in the Victorian mansion, Merchants Hall on Clifton Down Road; a few doors away from the Mansion House. Membership is by invitation only.

The Merchant Venturers's past leaves an indelible smear on their name. Following the disposal of Edward Colston's statue into the docks in June 2020 the Society made an unprecedented, and long overdue, statement. The Society tweeted:

'*To build a city where racism and inequality no longer exist, we must start by acknowledging Bristol's dark past and removing statues, portraits and names that memorialise a man who benefitted from trading in human lives.*'

It was a start. Let's see what happens next.

www.merchantventurers.com contains information about activities and short biographies of its members.

ENDNOTES

1. *Adam's Chronicle of Bristol*, 1910, Bristol, p.21.
2. Manson, M., *Bristol Beyond the Bridge*, Past & Present Press, 2000, p.19.
3. Ralph, E., *Government of Bristol 1373-1973*, 1973, Bristol, p.5.
4. *Adam's Chronicle of Bristol*, op.cit., p.95.
5. Dermott Harding, M., *Bristol Charters 1155 -1373*, 1930, Bristol Record Society, p.155.
6. Ralph, E., op cit, p.57.
7. Bettey, J.H., *The Landscape of Wessex*, 1980, Moonraker Press, p.100.
8. Quin, P., *The Holy Wells of Bath And Bristol Region*, 1999, Logaston Press, p.147.
9. ibid, p.149.
10. Ibid, p.9.
11. Evans, J., *A Chronological Outline of the History of Bristol*, 1824, Bristol, p. 92.
12. Legg, R., *Steepholm - Allsop Island*, 1992, Wincanton, p.20.
13. https://cardiffharbour.com/flatholm/#1488978342717-6b6c84df-5158 Accessed 15/02/2020.
14. Ralph, E., op. cit., p.7.
15. Evans, J., op. cit., p.262.
16. Arrowsmith Ltd, *Official Guide to the City of Bristol*, 1921, p.40.
17. Quin, P., *The Holy Wells of Bath And Bristol Region*, 1999, Logaston Press, p.109.
18. Williams, M., *Civic Treasures of Bristol*, 1984, City of Bristol, p.18.
19. Walker, D., *Bristol in the Early Middle Ages*, 1971, Bristol Branch of the Historical Association, p.8.
20. Quin, P., op. cit., p.176.
21. ibid, p.103.
22. *Adam's Chronicle of Bristol*, 1910, op. cit., p.72.
23. Evans, J., op. cit., p.121.
24. ibid., p.135.
25. ibid., p.216.
26. Seyer, S., *Memoirs Historical and Topographical of Bristol*, 1823, Bristol, p.51.
27. ibid., p.53.
28. Atkins, R., (ed. Young, P.) *Military Memoirs of the Civil War*, 1968,
Archon, p.46.
29. A Fellow of Queens College in Oxford, *The Sieges of Bristol in the Civil War*, 1868, Lewis and Taylor, p.32.
30. Ralph, E., *The Streets of Bristol*, 2001 (reprint), Bristol Branch of the Historical Association, p.10.
31. Evans, J., op. cit., p.283.
32. ibid., p.257.
33. Poole, S. and Rogers, N., *Bristol from Below*, 2017, The Boydell Press, p.182.
34. Evans, J., op.cit., p.273.
35. Sherborne, J.W., *The Port of Bristol in the Middle Ages*, 1971, Bristol Branch of the Historical Association, p.1.
36. Evans, J., op. cit., p.65.
37. ibid., p.145.
38. ibid. p.547.
39. Seyer, S., op. cit., p.544.
40. Evans, J., op. cit., p.247.
41. Mount, H., *A Lust for Window Sills*, 2008, London, p.357.
42. Ralph, E., *Government of Bristol 1373-1973*, 1973, Bristol, p.22.
43. Gomme, A. and Jenner, M., *An Architectural History of Bristol*, 2011, Oblong Creative, p. 262.
44. Merritt, D. and Greenacre, F., *Public Sculpture of Bristol*, 2011, Liverpool University Press, p.77.
45. ibid., p.79.
46. Anon, *Council House Bristol 1956*, Bristol. Unpaginated commemorative brochure.
47. ibid.
48. Bristol Post, 20 November 2012.
49. Merritt, D. and Greenacre, F., op. cit., p.49.
50. Hutton, S., *Bristol and its Famous Associations*, 1907, Arrowsmith, p.327.
51. Merritt, D. and Greenacre, F., op. cit., p.50.
52. Steeds, M. & Ball, R., *From Wulfstan to Colston*, 2020, Bristol Radical History Group, p.125.
53. https://www.merchantventurers.com/ Accessed 19/02/2020.

LAW AND ORDER

AN INTRIGUING DETERRENT TO PROSTITUTION
- The Courts -

At the end of the fifteenth century there were at least seven different courts presiding in Bristol to deal with a range of offences and judgements.[1]

- **The Court of Pie Poudre**. For instant settlement of disputes at fairs. *Pie poudre* derives from French for dusty feet!
- **The Tolzey Court**. For the speedy settlement of various civil actions typically related to market day. Usually held at the Guildhall.
- **The Staple Court**. For disputes over the sale of woollen cloth.
- **The Court of the Mayor and Sheriff**. For less serious cases such as drunkenness and bad language.
- **The Quarter Sessions**. Held every four months. The most serious cases were referred to the Court of Assize.
- **The Court of Assize**. Periodic criminal courts for the most serious cases. The visiting judge could order capital punishment.
- **The Court of the Admiralty**. Dealt with obstructions in the river, wrecks and royal fish. Since the reign of Edward II (1307 - 27), whales and sturgeon washed up on the shore have become property of the monarch. This is still the case. The court was abolished in 1835.

Pie Poudre Court, Stag and Hounds, Old Market

The Stag and Hounds, with its distinctive Doric columns and overhanging first floor, stands on the site of an old court house mentioned as being in existence in 1373. Although the Pie Poudre Court last officially sat in 1870 (in the spacious upstairs front room) the annual opening proclamation of the Court continued until 1970. On 30 September each year the court would be declared open and then immediately adjourned for refreshments in the bar downstairs.

The Stag and Hounds, Old Market, stands on the site of an old court house mentioned as being in existence in 1373.

Opening of the Pie Poudre Court, c.1950s.
On 30 September each year the court would be declared open and then immediately adjourned for refreshments in the bar downstairs.

Bye Laws

The following bye laws were proclaimed in the *Little Red Book of Bristol*, begun in 1344.[2]

- That no one wander by night about the town after sound of curfew unless he carry a lighted candle under pain of punishment.
- If any priest being in the service of any burgess shall be publically taken in fornication let him be removed immediately.
- That no one of whatsoever condition shall be throw urine or stinking or fouled water in the streets out of a window or door.
- That no one occupy the highways or lanes in the town or suburb of Bristol with dung, rubbish or timber.
- That no lepers hereafter stay in the town under pain of punishment.

There was an intriguing deterrent to prostitution. The doors and windows of the house of a 'common woman' would be removed and taken to the parish constable for storage. Only when the woman of 'ill repute' had left the premises would the fittings be returned.[3]

BRUTAL ENTERTAINMENT FOR HARSH TIMES
- Punishment -

Before the time when offenders were locked away in prison, the law had to be seen to be done. Punishment was public and humiliating. Hangings drew large crowds, offering brutal entertainment for harsh times.

Ducking Stool
The ducking stool first appeared in the sixteenth century. It was a cruel and degrading chastisement, The accused, invariably a woman, was tied to a chair and submerged, usually three times, until she was at the point of drowning. Suspected witches, prostitutes and 'scolds' (the patriarchal term for an opinionated woman) were the usual victims. The ducking stool was situated on the north bank of the Frome at Broad Weir. (Now covered-up; though the sluice gates for the River Frome can still be spied behind sturdy gates under a wall adjoining Castle Park.) The last recorded employment of Bristol's ducking stool was in 1718,[4] though, nationally, they were in use until the nineteenth century.

Stocks
Stocks were maintained in every parish for the punishment of petty offences such as non payment of fines, drunkenness and swearing. The last recorded use was in 1826, when two men were held for three hours in the stocks on Redcliffe Hill for drunkenness in the nearby churchyard.[5]

Whipping
Whipping was the punishment for those convicted of cheating or petty thieving. The

Whipping was the punishment for those convicted of cheating or petty thieving.

accused, both men and women, would be stripped to the waist and manacled to one of the city's several whipping posts and 'whipped until the blood comes'. Alternatively, they would be tied to the back of a cart and whipped through the streets – usually on a market day.

In 1705, a man, sentenced for stealing a cheese, was flogged from All Saints Church to the White Horse Inn, Redcliffe Street and then back to Newgate. The stolen cheese was exhibited by his side so that spectators were aware of his crime.[6]

In August 1747, Christopher Bragg, Mary Swain and Mary Cross were convicted of petty larceny; 'Let them be publickly whipt on

Temporary stocks in use at the base of the High Cross. From Millerd's map of Bristol – 1723 edition. Bristol Record Society.

Memorial on the wall of Cotham Parish Church to five men 'who were burned to death on the spot on which this chapel now stands'.

Saturday next'.[7]

Offenders in the Army or the Navy were flogged with a cat-o-nine-tails. Flogging could be severe enough to cause death. In 1731, a sergeant in the Fusiliers was sentenced to receive 2,000 lashes for desertion and fraud.[8] After a public outcry the sentence was remitted. The prisoner was stripped to the waist, a halter was put round his neck and he was drummed out of the city.

The public whipping of women was abolished in 1817 and that of men ended in the early 1830s, though it was not formally abolished until 1862.

Gallows

Gallows were placed by the prominent roads into Bristol. For the more extreme crimes bodies were left to rot, hanging in gibbet cages: a stark reminder that citizens should be law-abiding. These gruesome mementoes would be left swaying in the wind for many years, their unburied souls wandering forever.

Those convicted of the most serious offences, treason or anything that threatened the position of the monarch, were not only hung but also disembowelled and then cut into quarters – the head being placed on a spike. These grisly remains were left on show at the city gates.

Bristol escaped lightly when Judge Jeffreys (1645-89), the hanging Judge, visited Bristol after the Duke of Monmouth's pitchfork rebellion in 1685. Monmouth (1645-85), an illegitimate son of Charles II (1660-85), attempted to gather support in the West Country for an ill-fated attempt to overthrow James II (1685-88). His raggle-taggle followers were miserably defeated on Sedgemoor in Somerset.

Judge 'he'll rip yer guts out and show them to you afterwards' Jeffreys had already hung

LAW AND ORDER

114 people in the South West. In Bristol, he condemned six men to death. One of those sentenced, Edward Tippet, said he'd only gone to see what was happening. 'He never had any aims to wrong any person in life or estate.' They were hung on Redcliffe Hill. After the hanging, the bodies were drawn and quartered and the remains put on display.[9] It was an unambiguous warning of the fate of those who rebelled. Or even dared to think about rebellion.

Counterfeiting money was another capital offence. Indeed, anything remotely to do with forgery of coins was perilous. In 1479, Robert Markes was hanged and quartered in Bristol for making false accusations that Robert Strange was illegally coining fake money.[10]

Condemned felons, with a halter round their neck, would be taken from Newgate Gaol in a slow procession through the streets to their place of hanging. It was a highly visible warning. Spectators would come from far and wide to witness the scene. An estimated 30,000 people came to see the execution of a forger, William Carter, in 1816.

Between 1688 and 1802 the number of offences made punishable by death trebled. In the mid-eighteenth century England had the reputation of sending to the gallows more people per population than any other country in Europe. Stealing goods worth five shillings or more from a commercial property or forty shillings from a private house was a capital offence.[11] In some cases, after execution, the bodies were delivered to the local surgeon 'to be dissected and anatomised'.

In Bristol gallows were placed at:
- St Michael's Hill
- Redcliffe Hill
- Pembroke Road, Clifton. Formerly known as Gallow's Acre Lane – on the triangle of grass adjacent to the Downs.

As a punishment for blasphemy, James Naylor had his tongue pierced with a red hot iron, was branded with a B on his forehead and whipped through the streets of Bristol.

- Lawford's Gate, Old Market.

Temporary gallows were also erected in prominent spots. In 1601 a temporary gallows was built in the High Street for the execution of three soldiers, one of whom was reprieved at the last moment.[12]

The last execution in Bristol was in 1963 at Horfield Prison. 23-year-old Russell Pascoe was hung for his part in the murder of William Rowe, a Cornish farmer. Capital punishment in the United Kingdom was abolished two years later.

Transportation

Transportation, introduced around 1670, was seen as a more humane alternative to capital punishment. Before 1776, all criminal transportation – usually for seven years, though sometimes fourteen and occasionally for life – was to North America and the West Indies. Between 1727 and 1776, over 750 men

chapel now stands'.

While Henry VIII (1491-1547) banished Catholicism, Queen Mary (1553-58), his first daughter by Catherine of Aragon (1485-1536), was a fervent advocate of the Church of Rome. 'Bloody' Mary displaced, imprisoned and burned protestant bishops across the country including Thomas Cramner (1489-1556), the Archbishop of Canterbury.

Fox's *Book of Martyrs* gives vivid details of the Bristol burnings. William Saxton was cheerful to the last, while Richard Sharp, a humble weaver from Redcliffe, died 'denying the sacrament of the altar to be the body and blood of Christ', calling it an 'idol'.[14]

Other punishments

While fines were imposed for lesser offences there were other punishments such as 'Publicly burnt in the hand' (branded with a red hot iron on the thumb). Jonathan Chaney, found guilty of manslaughter in 1752, had this punishment inflicted upon him and was marked for life.[15] As was Sarah Morris in 1777, who was convicted of larceny.[16] Additionally, Morris had to endure six months hard labour in the Bridewell.

In 1646, the 'mad messiah' James Naylor, as a punishment for blasphemy, had his tongue pierced with a red hot iron, was branded with a B on his forehead and whipped through the streets on Bristol.[17]

In 1601, the Witchcraft Act was passed. Witchcraft was not primarily associated with the worship of the devil but more to do with the supposed power to do harm. In 1624, in Bristol, two people were hung for witchcraft, two for murder and two for 'un-natural practices'.[18] The Witchcraft act was repealed in 1736.

The 'mad messiah' James Naylor.

and women were transported from Bristol.[13] (Though not all of them were Bristolian.) After that date, with American Independence, transportation was to Australia and Van Dieman's Land (Tasmania). Transportation was abolished in 1868.

Burning

This punishment was reserved for the worst offenders: those accused of witchcraft or the heresy of subscribing to the wrong brand of Christianity.

In Bristol, there is a memorial on the wall of Cotham Parish Church to five men 'who were burned to death on the spot on which this

'A PERFECT COMMAND OF TEMPER'
- The policing of Bristol -

Bristol's first official police force was established in 1836.[19] Prior to this the maintenance of law and order was in the hands of householders. Each parish was expected to provide a parish constable and a nightly watch, either by doing it themselves or by hiring a watchman.

The parish constables were part-time and unpaid. Needless to say they were pretty useless. Even worse were the local watchmen, the Charleys, a figure of fun, usually too old for the job, and often drunk. Matters came to a head with the Bristol riots of 1831 when the Corporation came to the terrifying conclusion that they were at the mercy of the mob. Their last resort was to call in the militia, not an action that could always be relied upon. (In theory the War Office in London would have to approve such a request – a process that could take several days, by which time the ruckus would have taken its course!) A similar situation had occurred with the protests around the Bristol Bridge tolls in 1793. Then, the parish constables had either refused to attend the disturbance or had quietly melted into the crowd.[20]

It was obvious that some sort of paid-for policing was required. Cost was, of course, an issue as was the fear of a powerful despotic police force. Robert Peel (1788-1850) had already established his *Peelers* in London in the 1820s. It was time to follow suit.

Bristol was divided into four policing regions: Central, with a police station in the old guard house in Wine Street; Clifton with a station on Jacob's Wells Road; Bedminster

1950s Police Officers modelling the uniform worn by the 'new' Bristol Police Force from 1836 to 1850.

By 1918 there were 13 uniformed women on the beat, though women were not given the powers of a fully fledged constable until 1931.

Police dog Kyloe shortly before leaving the force in November 1960 to join handler PC Derek Johnston when he got a job with the Qatar Police. Kyloe was sold for 250 guineas and the Bristol Watch Committee conceded that one could not go without the other.

with a station on Bedminster Parade and St Philip's & Jacob's with a station opposite Trinity Church.[21]

Each station was run by an inspector supported by six sergeants and up to 50 constables. Even though there were plenty of applicants for these new jobs, finding the right quality of person was challenging. There were complaints about wrongful arrest, assault and general ineptitude.[22] One new recruit was dismissed for 'being in a brothel in Tower Lane, in a uniform'.[23] A regulation book was drawn up which suggested that the most valuable asset for a constable was 'a perfect command of temper'.[24] Constables were to patrol fixed routes at a stipulated speed. And so, the reassuring 'bobby on the beat' was born.

In 1844, the Wine Street Central Police Station was moved to larger, more suitable, premises opposite the Old Bridewell Gaol.[25] In the same year the River Police were formed to prevent theft from boats and general misbehaviour around the docks. By 1881 they had their own steam driven boat, *The River Queen*, which was also equipped for fire-fighting.[26]

The Bedminster Police Station was extended and rebuilt in 1880. The new station, designed by Henry Crisp and George Oatley and loosely inspired by Carisbrooke Castle, was an imposing fortress-style building with a central castellated tower built round a large courtyard.[27] Over time, additional police stations were opened: St George in 1869; Redland in 1890; Horfield (with an adjoining yard for stables and a fire engine) in 1903.[28]

Sometimes four legs are better than two. In 1889, the Mounted Section – horses are highly visible and are particularly good for crowd control – was added. And, many years later, in 1957, the first police dogs used to detect illegal substances and apprehend suspects, Kudos and Kyloe, joined up.

During the First World War female clerks were employed for the first time. By 1918 there were 13 uniformed women on the beat, though women were not given the powers of a fully fledged constable until 1931.

LAW AND ORDER

In 1928, the Central Police Station expanded onto land facing Nelson Street.

Rather than the traditional blue light, the police station was fronted by two curious cast iron lamp posts.

Bedminster Police Station, 1880. Architects Henry Crisp and his eighteen year old apprentice George Oatley. The building was inspired by Carisbrooke Castle.

In 1928, the Central Police Station expanded onto land facing Nelson Street. Rather than the traditional blue lamp, this austere and authoritarian Bath stone building was fronted by two cast iron lamp posts that have a touch of classical Rome, or maybe even a whiff of Italian fascism.

Speedy communication is the key to effective policing. In the early days the simple police whistle was used to summon support. By 1932 police telephone pillars (unfortunately, not the Dr Who style telephone box) were in use, while in 1946 the emergency 999 system was introduced. In 1968 personal radios were issued to officers.

Meanwhile, the new 1930s housing estates of Knowle West and Southmead were also provided with police stations. After the Second World War several specialist units were established including: Criminal Investigation Department (CID); the South Western Forensic Science Laboratory; Fingerprint Branch; Special Branch and the Photographic Department.[29]

In 1974, the Avon and Somerset Constabulary was formed. By the beginning of the twenty-first century the idea of the 'bobby on the beat' had fallen out of favour (with the police brass), while centralisation of police stations continued apace. The Nelson Street police station closed in 2005 and moved to a new building in Rupert Street, just 100 metres away.

In 2007, the buildings of the Nelson Street police station, the Bridewell, were taken over by *Artspace Lifespace* for use as a community arts centre, now called *The Island*.

ENDNOTES

1. Ralph, E., *Government of Bristol 1373-1973*, 1973, Corporation of Bristol, p.6.
2. Fleming, P. & Costello, K., *Discovering Cabot's Bristol*, 1989, Redcliffe, p.23.
3. Evans, J., *A Chronological Outline of the History of Bristol*, 1823, p.85.
4. ibid, 259.
5. Latimer, J. *Annals of Bristol in the Nineteenth Century*, 1887, Bristol, p.117.
6. ibid. p.66
7. Lamoine, G., *Bristol Gaol Delivery Fiats 1741-1799*, 1989, Bristol Record Society, p.7.
8. Latimer, op. cit., p.180.
9. Evans, J., op. cit., p.240.
10. ibid p 115.
11. Lamoine, G., op.cit., p.xiii.
12. *Adam's Chronicle of Bristol*, 1910, Arrowsmith, p.159.
13. Poole, S. & Rogers, N., *Bristol from Below*, 2017, Boydell Press, p.58.
14. Powell, K.G. *The Marian Martyrs and the Reformation in Bristol*, 1972, Bristol Branch of the Historical Association, p.14.
15. Lamoine, G., op. cit., p.11.
16. ibid p.42.
17. Seyer, S., *Memoirs of Bristol*, 1822-1825, Bristol, p 483-96.
18. Evans, J. op. cit., p.173.
19. Walters, W., *The Establishment of the Bristol Police Force*, 1975, Bristol Branch of the Historical Association, p.1.
20. Manson, M., *Riot! The Bristol Bridge Massacre of 1793*, third edition 2016, Tangent Books, p.62.
21. Walters, W., op. cit., p.9.
22. ibid p.14.
23. ibid p.12.
24. ibid p.11.
25. Latimer, J. op.cit., p.216.
26. http://british-police-history.uk/show_nav.cgi?force=bristol_river&tab=0&nav=alpha. Accessed 22/02/2020
27. Foyle, A. & Pevsner, N., *Somerset: North and Bristol*, 2011, Yale University Press, p.413.
28. Anon., *Arrowsmith's Dictionary of Bristol*, 1906, Arrowsmith, p.322.
29. https://www.avonandsomerset.police.uk/about/history-of-the-force/ Accessed 05/01/2020.

PRISONS

CASTLES, GATEHOUSES AND DUNGEONS
- Bristol's prisons -

Until the late eighteenth century prison was used only to hold people before their trial, or pending their sentence, as most criminals were punished by execution, corporal punishment, fines or transportation.[1] The only people to be held for long periods were debtors and then no allowance was made for feeding the prisoner. Debtors were to stay in prison until the liability was cleared; a difficult task to achieve while locked up. Those incarcerated relied on friends and family for food. Otherwise there was a charity box for donations by the entrance to the Newgate Gaol.

Prisons needed to be located in secure buildings – castles, gatehouses and cellars were particularly suited to the task. Parish lockups – one small secure room with no facilities – such as the lockup in Picton Street, Montpelier, were used for the overnight detention of drunks. A charter from Edward III dated 1347 gave Bristol the right to erect

Lock-up, Picton Street, Montpelier. 1828-32. Used for the overnight detention of drunks.

a cage for the incarceration of 'evildoers and disturbers of the peace found wandering in the City by night'. The letter C of the charter contains a lively illustration of a man being pushed into a hut no bigger than a dog kennel. The charter also empowered the city to punish bakers found guilty of short-changing by dragging them through the streets on a hurdle.[2]

- Newgate Gaol -

Originally part of the Bristol Castle precinct, Newgate was the city's earliest gaol. (Coincidentally, London's main gaol was also called Newgate.) It was first mentioned in 1148 and rebuilt in 1691. The worst offenders were kept in 'the pit'; not so much a gaol more a small underground dungeon with just one tiny window.

Prisoners relied on charity for food, fuel and straw for bedding. In the sixteenth century market traders were taxed to pay for the support of the inmates. It was revealed, however, in 1517 that the gaoler was pocketing this money for himself.[3]

In 1775, the prison reformer, John Howard (1726 - 90), vividly described the whitewashed Newgate building as 'white without, foul within'.[4] Prisoners were 'allowed a pennyworth of bread a day before trial and two pennyworth on conviction'.

Newgate Gaol was closed in 1820 and its inmates were transported by wagon to the recently built New Gaol on The Cut.

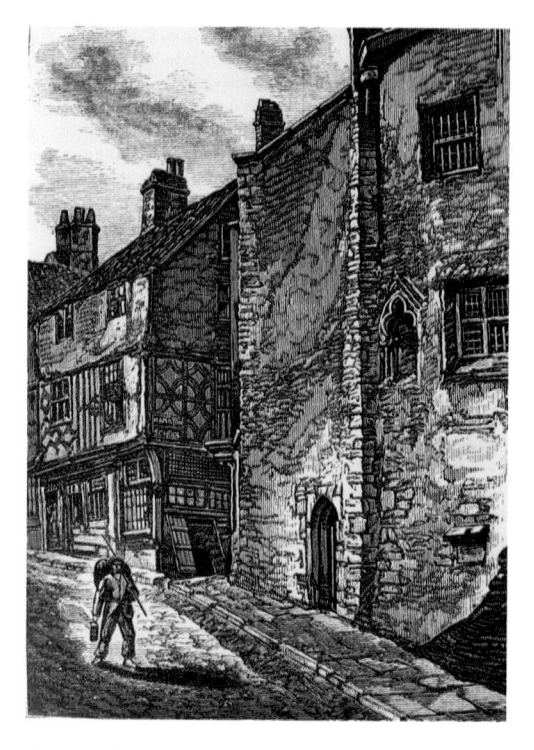

Newgate Gaol. There was charity box for donations by the entrance to the gaol.

- Bridewell -

According to John Howard, the Bridewell was equally as bad as Newgate. The Bridewell was established in the Middle Ages as a 'house of correction' where vagrants were set to hard labour breaking stones and undertaking other menial tasks. In 1807, rats were so rampant that a cat had to be kept in each cell to stop the vermin nibbling the prisoner's feet.[5] A report of 1813 stated that 'it was almost impossible for any building to be worse calculated for its purpose'.[6] It stood a while longer, but was eventually condemned as unsuitable and pulled down in 1865.

- Lawford's Gate Gaol -

Lawford's Gate Gaol. Built in 1791, it was severely damaged by fire in the 1831 riots and ceased to be used as a gaol in 1860.

Standing at the east end of Old Market, Lawford's Gate Gaol was 500 metres outside the city and was, in fact, in Gloucestershire. Built in 1791, it was severely damaged by fire in the 1831 riots and ceased to operate as a gaol in 1860. Part of the building and cells were used for Petty Sessions until it was demolished in 1907. Wessex House flats now stand on the site of the prison.

Women's cell at Lawford's Gate Prison. The Bristol Mercury reported 1 November 1892 the mysterious tale of the 'girl with no name'. 'As she was removed from the dock, there was on her face a smirk, which seemed to express her satisfaction at baffling the efforts of the magistrates, police and 200 inquiring individuals to find out who she is.'

- The New Gaol[7] -

By the latter part of the eighteenth century the law was becoming more punitive and larger prisons were required. In 1816, after a series of enquiries and reports, Bristol Corporation agreed that a new gaol should be built at a cost of £60,000. Land sandwiched between The Cut and the Floating Harbour was chosen for the site. The building of the gaol was finished in August 1820.

The New Gaol was a great advance on the buildings it superseded and was held as a model to be emulated across the country. It was designed to hold 197 prisoners, all to be kept in single cells measuring 6 feet by 9 feet. Facilities were such (and this was unusual) that the prisoners were expected to be able

The New Gaol was a great advance on the buildings it superseded and was held as a model to be emulated across the country. © Bristol Culture (Bristol Museum & Art Gallery).

to wash their hands and faces and comb their hair daily – and even bath once a month.

Their washing water came from a well, one hundred feet deep, the water being raised by a treadmill. The treadmill was a familiar feature of nineteenth century penal institutions. The New Gaol was equipped with treadmills for 20 people – besides drawing water the treadmills were also used for grinding corn.

Both sexes were held in the prison – but were to be strictly segregated. The female prisoners were supervised by a matron and no male warders were allowed to visit unless accompanied by the matron or another female officer.

The pennant stone gatehouse with its mock portcullis had a flat roof and a trap door designed specifically for executions. Executions were, of course, public affairs – and good crowd pullers at that. This could cause a problem as space for spectators was limited by the New Cut just across the road. At the first public execution, in 1821, of a young lad, John Horwood, sentenced for killing his girlfriend, notices were posted warning people to beware of being pushed into the unfenced river. Public executions were prohibited in 1849.

By 1840 conditions in the New Gaol had declined. A report by the visiting magistrates published in 1841 is reminiscent of the bad old days; much of the damage from the 1831 riots, when the gaol had been attacked and the prisoners released, had never been repaired. Conditions were overcrowded and unpleasant, and discipline was lax. The magistrates found the well water to be undrinkable, while the much vaunted availability of baths was non-existent. Many of the prisoners were poorly clothed against the winter cold and some even had no shoes. Also, due to the smallness of the windows, the air supply in the prison was static, the atmosphere consequently becoming stale and fetid. On the other hand many of the cells had unglazed iron windows with wooden shutters; in the winter the prisoners were compelled either to be shut in darkness or suffer the cold.

The magistrates also noted that the supervision of the prison at nighttime was difficult. The installation of gas lamps was therefore recommended. The segregation of the sexes had proved impossible. It was even claimed that two female prisoners had become pregnant by one of the warders – who had subsequently absconded.

The magistrates had already ordered food allowances to be increased: 'five ounces of dressed meat to be given twice a week, soup twice a week, and larger portions of bread when meat was not allowed.' Lest the magistrates were thought of as soft or extravagant, they felt compelled to point out that they were only meeting the requirements laid down by the Secretary of State, adding that due to this new dietary regime 'far less sickness is to be found in the prison'.[8]

Over the following years conditions continued to deteriorate. There was an increasing pressure of numbers on the gaol after the transportation to the colonies was abolished. In 1872 the Home Office complained to the Corporation that the prison was unfit for its purpose. The gaol was in such a state of decay that nothing could be done except to start building yet again. Accordingly, the Corporation bought land north of the city at Horfield Gardens but wisely procrastinated from doing anything further. Bristol was spared the expense of building another prison when, in 1877, the Home Office took over responsibility for penal institutions across the country.

All that remains of the New Gaol today is the flat roofed pennant stone gatehouse beside the Cumberland Road, and several metres of high grey wall. It is currently part of the Wapping Wharf development.

All that remained of the New Gaol in 1976 is the flat roofed gatehouse beside the Cumberland Road.

- Horfield -

After the 1877 Prison Act established a national prison service, a prison to serve the City and County of Bristol was built on the site of the Horfield pleasure garden. The new prison, based on a scaled down version of Pentonville in London, was opened in 1883. It had 160 cells. Each cell was built to standard prison size: 13ft long, 7ft wide and ten foot high.

There was a large wing for male prisoners, a smaller wing for women. The women wore striped blue and white dresses; the men had their heads shaved and wore ill fitting clothing with printed arrows. Women ceased to be held in Horfield in the 1920s.

Accommodation was increased by building new wings in the 1960s and 70s.

WHAT ARE THEY GOOD FOR?

- Prisoners of War -

What to do with prisoners of war? Nobody wants them, nobody wants to pay for their upkeep. Only a sense of humanity can save these unfortunates. After the demolition of Bristol Castle in 1654, there was no obvious place for the detention of captives. In 1665, 50 Dutch prisoners were held, of all places, in the crypt below the north transept of St Mary Redcliffe. The dark crypt was secure but conditions were unhealthy. Sanitation was make-shift and there was no space for prisoners to exercise. Four months later the prisoners were marched to more suitable accommodation in Chepstow Castle.[9]

French's Yard, a small enclosure off Guinea Street, in Redcliffe, was also used in the 1740s to hold French and Spanish prisoners. It was said, from the yard, there was access to Redcliffe caves. Security was lax. The yard was bounded by an easily scalable nine foot wall. On one occasion a group of Spaniards, who had been given leave to wash their clothes in the waters of Treen Mills, failed to return.[10] Even so French's Yard was used until the 1780s when prisoners were escorted to more secure premises at Knowle.

The Knowle Prison, on a site stretching from Rookery Road to Broadwalk, was established in 1744, when French prisoners were kept here. The site was also used during the Seven Years War (1756 - 63) when it is said that 1,700 people were incarcerated. It had to be abandoned when its water supply failed.[11]

A new stone prison with an outer perimeter wall was built in 1779, in Stapleton, on a bluff overlooking the River Frome. In 1780, 500 Spanish prisoners were marched from Portsmouth to Stapleton.[12] Shortly after, this number was swelled by another 400 Dutch – who brought their own bedding with them. Predictably, the prisoners were over-crowded and underfed. And because of the poor conditions, typhus and other diseases were a constant threat. The building was last utilised as a prison in 1814. After the peace-treaty of Paris, 2,000 prisoners were released. The buildings were later used for the Stapleton Workhouse.

ENDNOTES

1. Brodie, A., Croom, J. and Davies, J. *Behind Bars*, 1999, English Heritage, p.2.
2. Alexander, J. & Binski, P., (Ed) *Age of Chivalry*, 1987, Royal Academy of Arts, p. 277.
3. *Adam's Chronicle of Bristol*, 1910, Arrowsmith, p.83.
4. Latimer,J., op. cit., p.65.
5. ibid p.66.
6. ibid p.66.
7. Manson, M., *Bristol Beyond the Bridge*, 2000, Past & Present Press p.88-93.
8. *Report of the Visiting Justices into the Gaol and Bridewell of the City of Bristol*, 1841, p.5.
9. Nichols, J.F. and Taylor J., *Bristol Past and Present*, 1881, Bristol, Vol. 2, p.22.
10. Franklin, M., *Prisoners of War in Bristol* - Extracts from the Public Records Office, Greenwich, unpublished manuscript, Bristol Central Reference Library, B30152.
11. Vinter, D., *Prisoners of War near Stapleton Road, Bristol*. 1956, Bristol and Gloucester Archaeological Society -Transactions 1956, p.134.
12. ibid. 136.

A FRACTIOUS CITY

'THE POPULACE ARE LIKELY TO COLLECT TOGETHER IN MOBS ON THE SLIGHTEST OCCASION'

- Riots in the eighteenth century -

Bristol can be a fractious city. History has repeatedly shown that when Bristolians feel thwarted and have little recourse to justice they resort to mass civil protest. During the eighteenth century the crowd became increasingly vociferous about inequalities and incursions into their liberties. Hardly a decade went by when there wasn't a riotous demonstration of some sort. When prices go up, tensions go up quickly as well. A hungry population is a dangerous population. The price of bread, the fuel of life, was so important that it was controlled by the authorities.

There were food riots in 1709, 1753 and 1756; riots against religious dissenters in 1714; against Jews in 1753 and turnpike riots in 1727 and 1749. Protests against turnpikes revealed how vulnerable the city's elite were to the direct action of the people. New crimes such as the burning of toll gates were committed for which there were no judicial precedents. With

1831. A crowd went on the rampage, looting the Mansion House, besieging the prisons and burning down the Bishop's Palace.

a lack of effective policing those in authority had to develop new strategies to deal with large scale demonstrations. In just seven years (1728-35) the punishment for those pulling down toll gates increased from three months imprisonment, to seven years transportation, to death by hanging.[1]

The Queen Square riot of 1831. Three days of anarchy ended with the deaths of several hundred protesters.

The conflagration at Lawford's Gate Prison.

The century of rioting culminated with the Bristol Bridge riots of 1793 when the militia opened fire on a crowd of people, killing 14.

Yet the Bristol Bridge massacre was nothing compared to the Queen Square riots of 1831. Then, the arrival of the City's Recorder, Sir Charles Wetherall, set off a chain of events that was to lead to three days of anarchy and anger. Wetherall was unpopular on account of speaking against the 1831 Reform Bill, which would have sanctioned parliamentary reorganisation and wider voting rights. Other factors added to the lethal mix of discontent: a general dissatisfaction with a Corporation that was aloof and remote from the working classes, along with high unemployment. A crowd went on the rampage, looting the Mansion House, besieging the prisons and burning down the Bishop's Palace. They were all buildings symbolic of discontent with the establishment. With no effective police force the militia were eventually called in. The disturbances ended with the death of several hundred protesters – though the true figure has never been fully substantiated.

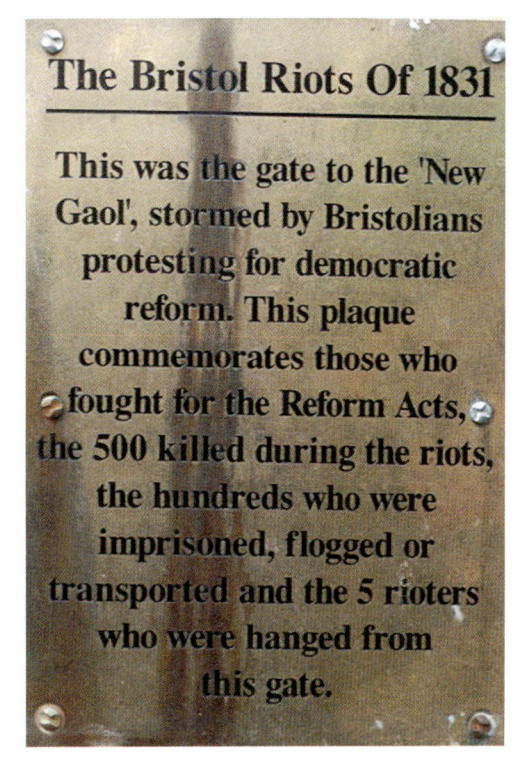

Unofficial sign marking the Bristol Riots of 1831.

WHEN RIOTS ROCKED OLD MARKET[2]
- Unemployment riots of 1932 -

During the 1930s the Government was concerned about the influence of communist agitators on the stability of the country.

In Bristol in 1932, at a time of high unemployment, there were a number of protest marches across the city. One such march led by the National Unemployed Workers Union (NUWU) on Pancake Day, 1932, led to what has been called the Old Market Riots.

The country was in the depth of the depression. Locally, nearly 28,000 people were registered at the six Bristol labour exchanges. To make matters worse, on 29 January 1932, the Public Assistance Committee, which was responsible for administering the unemployment relief, reduced unemployment benefit by 10%.

To protest against this cut in assistance the National Unemployed Workers Union proposed a march to the Council House, which was at that time on the corner of Corn Street and Broad Street. The police, however, forbade the protestors to approach the Council House and re-routed the march in the opposite direction to Old Market Street.[3]

At Old Market Street the police attempted to divert the crowd, which had grown to 4,000-5,000 people down a side road, Carey's Lane, next to the Empire Theatre. The police had broken the cardinal rule of crowd control: a crowd on the move needs somewhere to go. Mayhem ensued and because of the sheer number of people being forced down a bottleneck the police were jostled. The Chief Constable gave the order for batons to be drawn and the protestors charged.

Inspector Dyke, the policeman in charge at the scene, reported that 'sticks with nails protruding were being thrown at and used upon the police. I then gave instructions to the men who arrived with me to clear the street. The crowd was very hostile and it was impossible for any traffic to get away until the crowd was dispersed by the policemen using their sticks.'[4]

Inevitably bystanders were injured. One eye-witness reported 'The police on mounted horses and other police with batons charged us and drove us back into Old Market Street. Oh yes, people got hurt, people who weren't even in the scuffle. I can remember … a little lady there, there were a man and a woman there, they were clubbed down. They said they had just come from the pictures. And they had nothing to do with it.'

One policeman and several protestors were seriously injured though no arrests were made.

The dispersed crowd re-grouped at the Horsefair, where speeches were delivered. Police reinforcements from the nearby Bridewell police station were called and the demonstrators dispersed. Two people were arrested for disorderly conduct and assaulting police officers.

Many felt that the police had been too heavy-handed. Councillor H. E. Rogers (Bristol East Divisional Labour Party) wrote to Chief Constable Maby demanding disciplinary action be taken against the police who used unjustified violence. 'Surely your men have

Old Market demonstrations, 1932. The Chief Constable gave the order for batons to be drawn and the protestors charged.

not been instructed to trample to death law-abiding citizens whose only object is to pursue the legitimate conduct of citizens!'[5]

The Watch Committee concluded, however, that the police had acted with 'commendable restraint'.

Two weeks later, despite being refused permission by the police to march, the NUWU led another protest. Again the march ended in Old Market Street. The *South Gloucester Gazette* reported: 'At the unemployed headquarters at Shepherds Hall, over which continually floats the red flag, a posse of police barred the way. For a time the crowd halted, but eventually, urged on from the back, it advanced again, and the police drew batons in readiness. Immediately came a shower of missiles, half-bricks, coke, gas-piping and iron bars, all of which had been collected by the procession on route. Immediately the police charged and in a moment the demonstrators were scattering in all directions, those who stood their ground being speedily dealt with. Again and again the police swept through their ranks and two ambulances were soon busy carrying casualties to the Infirmary.'

Bill Curtiss, a participant, saw things differently: 'To the right hand side as we were facing Castle Street ... in the annex to the Empire Theatre...he (Chief Constable Maby) had two more motor coach loads of police there in reserve ... hiding in the annex and the theory was that if they came out from the annex and took the first dozen rows from behind they'd have the ring leaders and the the march would break up into disorder... which he wasn't very far wrong ... these other police piled out from the annex and took us from behind ... and of course right away you know a punch up started, people was getting whacked with the batons ... we was getting a right licking...'[6]

According to Bill Curtis the demonstrators grabbed anything that was at hand to use as missiles. Market stalls were raided, and potatoes and cabbages and coal were thrown at the police.

Photographs of the demonstration show policemen with truncheons beating marchers to the ground. Several bodies lie sprawled on the road, bicycles abandoned, placards discarded. At a press conference the next day Chief Constable Maby justified this brutal containment with a display of weapons – jemmies, batons, metal railings – allegedly taken from the protestors. He claimed that not more than 50 police were engaged in dispersing demonstrators. *The Bristol Evening World*, however, reported that nearly 300 police took part.

By now the disturbances in Bristol had drawn the attention of the Home Office, who made a 'telephonic inquiry' about the events.

Maby's subsequent report to the Home Office appeared to be more concerned with the interruption to the traffic than anything else. Maby succinctly described the events in Old Market; 'One procession proceeded through St Philips down Old Market Street, and another procession, at the same time, marched from the other end of Old Market Street. Causing serious congestion. A cordon of police was immediately lined up across Old Market Street and the marchers requested to stop. They refused and were told they would not be allowed to march any further and must disperse. The marchers then attacked the police with sticks and banners, pieces of iron, stones and other missiles and the inspector in charge gave orders for the police to draw their truncheons and disperse the crowd, and after a short time order was restored. The mounted police were called out, but did not draw their staves'.[7]

The protests continued throughout the spring of 1932. The police were less heavy handed, preferring to monitor the situation rather than wade in. Meanwhile, Chief Inspector Maby opened up correspondence with his counterpart in Manchester, Chief Constable Maxwell, where similar disturbances had occurred in Stevenson Square.

On 13 April 1932 Maby wrote to Maxwell: 'I believe that time has come to say 'stop' and proceedings are therefore being instituted against some of the communist speakers.'[8] Maby was certainly overstepping the mark of non-political policing. Fortunately the unemployment situation began to improve. By 1937 there were 11,500 people registered as unemployed in Bristol.[9] It was boom time again, largely helped by the rise of the aeroplane manufacturing industry.

A PEACEFUL PROTEST

- The Bristol Bus Boycott -

Of course, protest marches and rioting aren't the only way of expressing frustration and displeasure.

On 28 August 1963 150,000 black and white Americans marched on Washington D.C. in the biggest civil rights demonstration ever seen.[10] On the same day in Bristol it was reported that the 'colour bar' on those working on the buses had been lifted.

Even though there was a shortage of bus conductors the Bristol Omnibus Company – jointly administered by Bristol City Council – had previously refused to recruit black applicants.

When Guy Bailey turned up for an interview he overheard the following:

'Your two o'clock appointment is here, and he's black.'

The Bristol bus boycott was a significant step forward for improved race relations in the UK. Mural at the end of Byron Street, St Paul's, featuring Roy Hackett by Michele Curtis and Paintsmiths.

'Tell him the vacancies are full,' came the reply. 'We don't employ black people.'

A group of West Indians including Roy Hackett, Owen Henry, Peter Carty, Guy Bailey and others, together with black youth worker Paul Stephenson, campaigned to highlight and defeat this racial injustice through a bus boycott.[11]

At first the Transport and General Workers Union appeared to be shamefully complicit with the bus company.[12] Some black churches didn't want to 'ripple the water' by being involved in such confrontational action.

Pressure mounted and a national debate opened up. 'I shall stay off the buses,' Tony Benn (1925-2014) the MP for Bristol South East announced.[13] Harold Wilson (1916-95), the then Leader of the Opposition, wished the campaign every success.

After four months of negotiation, on the very day that Dr Martin Luther King Junior (1929-68) declared 'I have a dream', the bus company acquiesced. 'There will be complete integration without regard to race, colour or creed,' said Ian Patey, the Bus Company's general manager. 'The only criterion will be the person's suitability for the job.'[14]

This wasn't the end of the problem. Recruitment of West Indian and Asian staff to the buses was slow, and integration an on-going issue. Nevertheless, the Bristol bus boycott was a significant step forward for improved race relations in the UK; Britain's first Race Relations Act was introduced two years later, in 1965.

In 2009 Paul Stephenson[15] was awarded an OBE for his services to equal opportunities, and to community relations in Bristol.

ENDNOTES

1. Poole, S. & Rogers, N., *Bristol from Below*, 2017, Boydell Press, p.171.
2. This article first appeared in Burton, E. and Manson, M. *Vice and Virtue - Discovering the History of Old Market*, 2015, Bristol Books, p. 30-3.
3. Backwith, D. and Ball, R., *Bread or Batons*, 2012, Bristol Radical History Pamphleteer Pamphlet #19, p.16.
4. Report by Inspector A Dyke. 10 February. Bristol Archives, POL/20/9/2.
5. Letter from H.E. Rogers to Chief Constable 11 February 1932. Bristol Archives PLO/20/9/2
6. Interview with Bill Curtis, 11/11/1998. https://sounds.bl.uk/Accents-and-dialects/Millenium-memory-bank/021M-C0900X00510X-2600V1
7. Report by F.W. Hicks, Superintendent and Chief Clerk, undated, Bristol Archives, POL/20/9/2.
8. Letter from Maby to J. Maxwell. 13/4/1932, Bristol Archives, POL/20/9/2.
9. Tout, H., *The Standard of Living in Bristol*, 1938, University of Bristol Social Survey, p.12.
10. Dresser, M., *Black and White on the Buses*, 1986, Bristol Broadsides, p. 47.
11. ibid., p.7.
12. ibid., p.12.
13. ibid., p. 26.
14. ibid., p. 47.
15. Stephenson, P., *Diary of a Black Englishman*, 2011, Tangent Books. p.119.

FIRE SERVICE

FIRE
- A constant threat -

Narrow streets and wooden houses made the likelihood of fire a constant threat. In 1237, the greater part of Bristol was burnt to the ground. From the earliest days thatched buildings were forbidden, while prominent citizens were required to keep leather buckets in their houses.[1] If fires got out of control in the tightly packed streets there was little that could be done. About the only way to prevent the spread of a conflagration was the drastic measure of pulling down neighbouring dwellings.

In 1584, adjoining buildings were pulled down on the Quay Head when a house was set fire by a candle that had unwisely been left burning on a barrel of pitch. 'The smoke was so thick over the city that no one could see the skies.'[2]

The Great Fire of London in 1666, which raged for five days and destroyed five sixths of the capital, was a lesson for all. Building regulations were tightened. In Bristol, many industries such as sugar boiling, glass making,

Horse drawn fire engine late 1800s/early 1900s.

brewing and distilling were potential fire risks. In 1682, the house of Abraham Nichols, a 'strong water man', caught on fire in Broad Street. The gutters were alight with flaming brandy. Two houses on each side were also damaged.[3]

The first fire engine in Bristol – a mobile tank and pumping device – was purchased in 1647.[4] In 1717, it was recommended that each ward should have a 'fireman' who would be equipped with two buckets, a pick hook and an axe. Four dozen buckets along with a hosepipe

Bristol Police Fire Brigade, 1906.

Early Sunday morning on 22 December, 1907 and a fire destroys most of the warehouse and offices of corn and flour merchants, Bodey, Jerrim and Denning Ltd. The fire float stationed at Prince Street Bridge was soon on the scene and stayed dousing the building until late in the afternoon.

were also kept at the Council House.[5] Buckets would be filled from the nearest water source and passed by hand in a human chain. In the face of a full emergency, such as when a sugar house burnt to the ground in 1762[6], this fire fighting equipment proved to be predictably inadequate.

In 1718, a number of merchants set up the Crown Insurance Fire Office. Their fire fighting team would only attend premises that displayed their insurance plaque.[7] If you weren't insured they wouldn't put out your fire. There was money to be made through firefighting and over the century other fire

FIRE SERVICE

Bridewell Fire Station decorated for the Coronation of King George V on 22 June, 1911.

insurance companies were established; New Bristol Fire Office, 1770; Bristol Universal, 1774.

The Bristol Corporation Fire Service, a citywide fire service managed by the police force, was formed in 1877. A sparkling new, fit-for purpose, steam engine, drawn by horses borrowed from the Bristol Tramways Company, was purchased and garaged next door to the recently rebuilt Bridewell Police Station.[8]

To enable improved coordination during the Second World War, the local fire services were integrated in 1941, into the newly established National Fire Service. Three years after the end of the war Bristol Fire Brigade once again became a separate entity. This time it was no longer part of the police force and run as an independent corporation department.

The Pyronaut

Bristol had its own specially designed fire boat, the Pyronaut (originally named Phoenix II). This low keeled boat, built by Charles Hill & Sons in 1933, hugs the water so that it can pass under any of Bristol's bridges without them opening. It can usually be seen moored outside M Shed.

ENDNOTES

1 Ralph, E. *Government of Bristol 1373-1973*, 1973, Bristol Corporation, p.14.
2 *Adam's Chronicle of Bristol*, 1910, Arrowsmiths, p.119.
3 Evans, J., *A Chronological Outline of the History of Bristol*, 1824, Bristol, p.229.
4 ibid., p.14.
5 Latimer, J. *Annals of Bristol in the Eighteenth Century*, 1893, Bristol, p.53.
6 ibid., p. 356.
7 Fire insurance plaques are now collector's items. At an auction in 2019 the mark for the Bristol Universal Fire Office with the stamped policy number 336 (c.1774) was sold for £4,400.
8 Latimer, J. *Annals of Bristol in the Nineteenth Century*, 1887, Bristol, p.484.

MANSON'S BRISTOL MISCELLANY

MAKING MONEY

SHIPSHAPE AND BRISTOL FASHION
- The port of Bristol in the Middle Ages -

By the twelfth century Bristol was a thriving port, trading locally, nationally and internationally. In 1164, it was written that 'Bristol is now full of ships from Ireland, Norway and every part of Europe, which brought hither great commerce and much foreign wealth'.[1] But the journey up the Avon to Bristol was, and still is, not straightforward.

There were two holding areas where ships would anchor while they waited to take on a pilot and catch the incoming tide. Kingroad was in the Severn at the mouth of the Avon. Foreign vessels were required to anchor at Kingroad while their papers were examined and customs and immigration formalities completed. Sometimes goods would be transferred to lighters.[2]

About a mile up-river from the mouth of the Avon was Hungroad, an area of relatively safe water on a gentle bend near Pill. Vessels would wait here for permission to proceed from the harbour master.

Once the tide was right ships, guided by the experienced pilots from Pill, would travel

In 1497, John Cabot set sail in his brave little ship.
Statue by Stephen Joyce, 1986, Narrow Quay.

A replica of the Matthew was built to mark the 500th anniversary celebrations of John Cabot sailing to North America. © Shawn Spencer-Smith

Twice a day the water receded rapidly, leaving the docks as no more than a 'soft and oozy' trench. Ships were frequently moored alongside the quay two deep[4] and unless they were securely tied-up, 'shipshape and Bristol fashion' cargoes could unbalance dangerously and 'keel over'.

Despite this difficult journey, Bristol was a popular port simply because it was safe. Its geographical position meant that no invaders or pirates were ever going to take it by surprise.

Equally important was that Bristol had a considerable hinterland for trading. There was access up the meandering Severn to Worcestershire and beyond, while the Bristol Channel opened up the markets of South Wales and the Somerset ports of Bridgwater, Dunster, Watchet and Minehead.

up the river, going with the flow, and complete their journey. Sailing the Avon, with its twists, turns and gorge was a tricky business. Many preferred not to use their sails and to be towed.[3] Some would transfer their cargoes into smaller boats which would then be hauled up the river from the shore by 'Pill Hobblers', sometimes using horses.

The Avon has a ferocious tidal range.

Bristol's overseas traders had a vast and ready market for their imports. Although he was writing about a later time, Daniel Defoe (1660-1731) was impressed by the scale of Bristol's trade. '...as they have a very great trade abroad, so they always have buyers at home, for their returns. And such buyers that no cargo is too big for them.'[5]

- Expanding the port -

The port was outstandingly successful – so much so that by the beginning of the thirteenth century the dock-side facilities were creaking at the seams. More water-frontage was needed. In 1239, a radical solution was found.

The plan was to divert the Frome from its original curving course along what is now Baldwin Street. A deep trench was to be dug across marshy land so that the river would flow directly south. It was a seven year project. At first, the people of Redcliffe, from across the river, stood back and watched, fearful that the new wharf would diminish their trade on Redcliffe Back. Eventually, King Henry III (1216-72), ordered the Redclivians to join in with the digging and shifting. The scheme was a resounding success. At a stroke Bristol had doubled the length of its quayside.[6] The new quay was reserved for international trade, while what was later to be called Welsh Back was set aside for local and coastal shipping.

Bristol was now entering one of its periods of epic vigour. The diversion of the Frome and the building of the Quay led the way to other great projects. Bristol's first stone bridge across the Avon was constructed in 1247 and, a few years later, the impenetrable Portwall, guarding Bristol south of the river, was built.

- Blankets and wine -

During the eleventh century Ireland was a major trading partner. Bristol had an unpleasant reputation for the dispatch of white slaves to Ireland. Though where these slaves came from is not clear. Wulfstan, the Bishop of Worcester (c.1008-95), successfully campaigned against this evil trade.[7] Imports from Ireland included fish, linen and canvas.

Until the export of wool was banned in 1337, in an attempt to encourage the home production of cloth, Cotswold 'golden fleeces' were a popular purchase with Flemish merchants. By 1360, 4,500 bolts of home woven woollen cloth were exported from Bristol annually. Admittedly, the cloth was not as fine as that produced by the Flemish weavers but the trade was a valuable one.[8] It is rumoured that local clothier Thomas Blanket was responsible for the development of the heavy bedding cloth that bears his name. Though, it has to be admitted, the evidence for this is tenuous.

Imports far outweighed exports.[9] The major overseas import was wine from Bordeaux in English-ruled Gascony. It was not an easy run – the Bay of Biscay was notorious for its choppy sea and also pirates.

In 1453, at the end of the Hundred Years War (1337-1453), Gascony returned to French rule. Bristolians subsequently sought sources of wine elsewhere and began to trade with the Iberian Peninsula. Alongside iron, woad, olive oil, dried fruit and almonds, medieval imports from Spain included some fantastically exotic produce: there was liquorice, saffron and beaver fur. In return, Bristol sent to Spain woollen cloth, tanned hides and animal pelts, lead and tin. Products from Portugal included Madeira wine, cork, and dried fruits such as figs and raisons.[10]

The quays were hectic with ships being loaded and unloaded and goods taken to storage sheds. Merchandise was carried in sacks or rolled in barrels; the first use of a crane is recorded in 1475. Keeping the quay tidy and usable for all was a constant problem. A particular quandary was the stacks of building wood piled high.[11] As well as ships from Bristol there were vessels from Ireland, Spain, Portugal, France and even Prussia. Bristol merchants did not hesitate to use these foreign ships to carry their own cargoes. Many languages could be heard, though foreign nationals were required to stay in designated lodgings.

Bristolians were always searching for new markets. By the 1450s we see the beginning of trade beyond Europe and the import of exclusive merchandise from much further afield. Ships were sailing to the Mediterranean in search of luxury goods such as Chinese silk and high-priced spices that had been traded in central Asia and brought along the Silk Road. There was also trade to the far north – including frequent trips to the 'costes colde' of Iceland.

Fish was a staple food; voyages in search of cod ventured further and further west. Indeed, there were rumours of a mysterious and misty land at what should have been the edge of the world.

In 1497, John Cabot (c.1450-98?) set sail in his brave little ship to seek a pioneering trading route to the east.[12] Instead, he came across a whole new – to Europeans, at least – continent blocking the way.[13]

'This year, on St John the Baptist's day (24 June 1497) the land of America was found by the Merchants of Bristowe, in a shippe of Bristowe, called the Mathew; the which said ship departed the port of Bristowe the second of May and came home again the 6 August next following.'[14]

There had long been whispers about such lands, with tales of cod-rich seas. The Vikings had spoken of Helluland, a place of large flat stones and Arctic foxes. Some say sailors had kept the knowledge of this mysterious and uninviting coast to themselves. But now the story was out of the bag.

The following year Cabot gathered together a flotilla of five ships and set off to explore further.

What happened next is uncertain. None of his fleet returned. Whether the ships were swallowed by the sea or his expedition was attacked by indigenous peoples, we do not know.

Maybe he settled in the New Found Land? Or perhaps, he did return, but this went unrecorded. The fate of the second expedition remains a compelling mystery

In fact, the 'discovery' of North America was all rather unsatisfactory. The 'Indians' weren't Indian; rather than exotic spices there was cod; and the hoped-for new market for woollen cloth was a disappointment. It would be another 150 years or so before North America was seen as being of any real value.

The majority of Bristol's shipping was, however, domestic. Trows negotiated the treacherous currents and shifting mudbanks of the Severn up to Gloucester and the heart of England, as well as the Wye as far as Monmouth. If the tide and weather was favourable, trows could sail from Kingroad to Gloucester in a day.[15] Coasters would ply the Devon and Somerset ports and sail to South Wales.

By 1500, Bristol had a population of around 9,500.[16] Today, in comparison, we would think of this as a small market town, similar in extent to, say, Devizes or Marlborough. Considering its size, the scale of Bristol's enterprise was indeed extraordinary.

- William Canynges the Younger -

There can be few people whose lives are commemorated by not just one altar tomb, but two – almost side by side. The first effigy in St Mary Redcliffe Church depicts Canynges (1402-74) in mayoral attire lying by his wife, Joan. Just metres away is another, plainer, figure showing Canynges in the robes of a priest.

As we have seen, the fourteenth and fifteenth centuries were a golden age for Bristol. Some merchants became fabulously wealthy. One such family was the Canynges. Three generations held the office of mayor. William Canynges the Younger was a true shipping magnate – he had a fleet of ten ships and according to a plaque in St Mary Redcliffe Church is said to have employed a workforce of over 800 people. He traded with Iceland, Scandinavia, Prussia, Gascony and the Iberian Peninsula.[17] On return journeys his ships, depending on where they came from, would be laden with wine, woad, iron, oil, wax, soap and fruit. Wind dried cod was a favourite import from Iceland and Scandinavia.

William Canynges the Younger was five times mayor and also represented Bristol in Westminster. Described by the chronicler William Worcester (c.1415-c.1482) as 'very rich and very wise'[18] he lived in a sumptuous house on Redcliffe Back – the earthen-ware tiled floor is preserved in the British Museum

During the fifteenth century St Mary Redcliffe was transformed from a humble Norman chapel to the glorious creation we see today.

(though not on display).

Along with other merchants, the Canynges family, were responsible for the rebuilding of St Mary Redcliffe Church.[19] If church building is seen as a barometer reflecting the state of the economy, trade must have been going well. During the fifteenth century St Mary Redcliffe was transformed from a humble Norman chapel to the glorious creation we see today. In 1445, when the church was nearing completion, the spire, nearly 300 feet of it, was blown down in a storm, causing it to come crashing through the nave. The nave was rebuilt, but the church spire remained truncated for 400 years until it was reconstructed in 1872.

At the age of 65, after a prosperous career, Canynges turned his back on the world of commerce. He sought holy orders and eventually became Dean of Westbury College, a few miles north of Bristol. He sang his first mass at St Mary Redcliffe on Whitsunday, 1468. This event is still commemorated annually by the attendance of the Lord Mayor and Corporation at the Whitsun Rush Sunday service when the floor, as tradition dictates, is strewn with rushes.

It is from Westbury that the plainer tomb came, transferred when Henry VIII closed the college in 1544.

The two faces of William Canynges the Younger. Canynges was a true shipping magnate – he had a fleet of ten ships and is said to have employed a workforce of over 800 people.

MAKING MONEY

A PLACE TO BUY AND SELL
- Markets -

As well as being an important port and river crossing, Bristol was a place to buy and sell.

Due to topography and chronology markets were scattered across the town. The most ancient market was along the wide and busy street that led from the Norman castle eastwards – the eponymous Old Market Street. Produce was sold from wooden standings (stands) lining the roadway.

By 1247, the main market, held on a Wednesday, had moved to the High Cross. There was also a Monday market, across the river, in Thomas Street in addition to a market in Temple Street. Not all goods were sold from stalls. Artisans and craftsmen making leather goods, cloths, baskets, household goods, bread and so on, traded from their workshops. Like London Bridge, Bristol Bridge was lined with shops, so much so that you could walk across the bridge without knowing. Rents here were higher than anywhere else.

Over the centuries specialist retail areas became established. This not only made shopping easier, it also kept quality up and prices down. Grouping together market traders of the same ilk ensured a genuine 'market economy'. In 1615, a fish market was built in the Shambles. The placing of a fish market is always tricky. Smells aside, fresh water and a facility to dispose of fish guts and other waste products are essential.

Having said that, stallholders were liable to set up shop wherever and whenever they could. In 1711, the Common Council became so exasperated with the nuisance created by

The celebrated architect John Wood was enticed from Bath to build the Corn Exchange.

The Corn Exchange. This substantial, classical style building fronting Corn Street housed the market for corn and flour.

unauthorised vegetable sellers in the central streets that they directed the traders to move their stalls to the quieter areas of Temple Street and Broadmead.[20] Additionally, market traders could be fined for staying open after the allotted hour of 6.00pm.[21]

Over the river, in Thomas Street, a new Thursday market was authorised in 1570, to alleviate the economic downturn cased by the

Behind the main body of the Exchange was St Nicholas Market where meat, poultry, dairy produce and vegetables were sold.

decay of the local woollen cloth industry. The market was for 'wool, woollen yarn, cattle and victuals...'.[22] Millerd's map of 1673 shows a flat roofed colonnade attached to St Thomas's Church. There were also four posts topped by brass caps – 'nails' – used for counting money. In 1673, a market for sheep, great droves of which came all the way from Wales, was held in a court adjoining St Thomas's Church.[23] Over the years the Thomas Street Market came to specialise in livestock. Its location, in such a confined area, was not ideal; the stink, the noise and the general confusion of pens for animals was a frequent cause of complaint.

In the early eighteenth century Daniel Defoe observed that the area around the High Cross, known as the *Tolzey*, was so crowded that it was a hindrance to business.[24] (The name *Tolzey* derives from toll. If you say *Tolzey* with a Bristol accent it kind of makes sense!) There was an attempt to remedy the situation when the celebrated architect John Wood (1704-54) was enticed from Bath to build the Corn Exchange. The foundation stone

The Corn Exchange's central courtyard, originally open roofed, was surrounded by a number of rooms used for public offices.

was laid in 1740. This substantial, classical style building fronting Corn Street housed the market for corn and flour. The Exchange's central courtyard, originally open roofed, was surrounded by a number of rooms used for public offices.[25] Behind the main body of the Exchange was St Nicholas Market where meat, poultry, dairy produce and vegetables were sold. While he was at it, Wood rebuilt the facade of the reputedly oldest tavern in Bristol, the Rummer, in All Saints Lane, whose history dates back to 1241.[26]

Cattle and sheep would be herded through the streets of the city and across Bristol Bridge.

Bristol Markets in 1793:[27]

1. **Meat, poultry and vegetables:** Exchange market, (St Nicholas Market, behind the Corn Exchange). Every day, except Sunday.
   The market consisted of three arcades. The arcade directly to the south of the Exchange was called the Gloucestershire Market, while the arcade that runs to the High Street was known as the Somerset Market.
2. **Corn:** Corn Exchange.
3. **General provisions:** St James's Market, Union Street. Every day for vegetables, Wednesday and Saturdays for meat.
4. **Fruit and vegetables:** east end of Old Market Street. Wednesday and Saturday. Fish was sold here on Monday, Wednesday and Saturday.
5. **Fish:** an unauthorised market along the quayside near St Nicholas Church. Every day, except Sundays.
6. **Live poultry and pig market:** Welsh Back, Wednesday. Also fruits and nuts in season.
7. **Cheese:** in the shade of Corn Market Lane, Wednesday and Friday.
8. **Live cattle, pigs, sheep and horses:** St Thomas Street Market, 'The Smithfield of Bristol', Thursday. Wool was sold in the adjacent Wool Hall.
9. **Hay:** Hay market, Broadmead. Tuesday and Friday.
10. **Raw and untanned hides.** The Leather Hall, near the Back. Wednesday and Saturday. On Thursdays tanned leather was sold.

MANSON'S BRISTOL MISCELLANY

Tolzey colonnade alongside All Saint's Church. All Saint's conduit to the right.

In 1830, fields to the south east of the city, Temple Meads, were bought for the establishment of a permanent market. With the opening of the Temple Meads Market the livestock market in Thomas Street was closed.[28] The Temple Meads site was not without problems though. Many animals arrived by ship. Livestock from Ireland was unloaded from the wharves near Hotwell Road. Cattle and sheep would then be herded through the streets of the city and across Bristol Bridge.

In 1845 a section of the Temple Meads land was purchased for the construction of Bristol's new railway station.

Markets and street traders come and go. The fruit and vegetable stalls in Old Market Street were closed in the 1950s. The wholesale fruit, vegetable and flower market moved in 1968 from St Nicholas Market to its current location in St Philips Marsh. The St Nicholas Street fish market, now a popular bar,

In 1905 the following markets are listed;[29]
- Cattle Market (Thursday): Temple Meads, east of Bath Bridge – hence Cattle Market Road.
- Cheese Market (Wednesday): Union Street.
- Corn and Flour Market (Tuesday and Thursday afternoons): Corn Exchange, Corn Street.
- Fish Market (open daily): St Nicholas Street.
- Hay and Coal Markets (Tuesday and Friday): St James's Church Yard – hence Haymarket.
- Hide Skin, Fat and Wool Market (Thursday and Saturday): Thomas Street – hence the Wool Hall, currently the Fleece and Firkin.
- Meat, Vegetables, Fruit and Cheese (Wednesday and Saturday): St James's Market, Union Street. Formerly an outdoor market, it was enclosed in 1858.

MAKING MONEY

The Nails were used as counting tables for the completion of money transactions. Hence the saying 'pay on the nail'.
Photo: Bristol Post.

was closed in the 1990s. Also in the 1990s a Wednesday 'Farmers Market' was established along Corn Street.

Meanwhile in the twenty-first century, artisan food traders, crafts people and booksellers are encouraged at weekends to line the walkway along the Watershed to give the area vibrancy and colour.

Nails

The Nails stand in Corn Street outside the Exchange. Made of brass, with their thick rims, these wonderful bulbous baroque pillars were used as counting tables for the completion of money transactions. Hence the saying 'pay on the nail'. Originally positioned 100 metres away in the Tolzey, they were gifts from Bristol merchants to the city and are dated 1595, 1625, 1630 and 1631. There was another set of Nails across the river outside St Thomas's Church – though these have long since disappeared.

THE SECULAR HIGHLIGHT OF THE YEAR

- Fairs -

While markets were an everyday event the fair was something special, bringing in people from the surrounding countryside. In seemingly simpler times the fair was the secular highlight of the year where more exotic and specialist produce could be bought, as well as enjoying travelling entertainments. There was a set calendar for fair people, who moved across the country from town to town between April and October. There are records of fairs in Bristol, usually held on saint's days, as early as the thirteenth century. The most important fair, certainly established by 1374,[30] was held for nine days in September in the spacious St James's Church yard. Though, with stands spilling out into adjacent streets, it frequently went on for several days longer.

In 1529, a smaller scale fair in Redcliffe was licensed to run annually at Candlemas.[31] It was short-lived, being cancelled in 1542[32]. Also in south Bristol was the St Paul's Fair, authorised in 1550, to be held in Temple Street for two days, 25-6 March.

The St James's Fair provided a useful income for the church. In 1684, rental of pitches generated over £80.00. In Victorian times the famous showman 'Lord' George Sanger wrote

The most important fair was held for nine days in September in the spacious St James's Church yard.
© Bristol Culture (Bristol Museum & Art Gallery).

'a charge of a guinea a foot was levied for the frontage of each show or stall, the money going to the clergy of St Mary Redcliffe'.[33]

Before the industrial revolution, fairs were a focal point for commerce. Heavily laden wagons from across the country brought all manner of goods to St James's Fair: textiles from the Midlands; cotton stockings from Tewkesbury; lace from Buckinghamshire, leather goods from London; hardware from Sheffield, Birmingham, Walsall and Wolverhampton and so much more.[34]

Visitors from across the South West poured into Bristol to buy from, or gaze at, these stands of unusual and exotic wares, alongside stalls hawking all manner of food and drink. There roundabouts, swings, pleasure wheels (a smaller, early version of the Ferris Wheel), puppet shows, peep shows, freak shows (the tallest man, the fattest man, the living skeleton, raw meat-eating cannibal twins[35]), acrobats and exotic animals. At times credibility was stretched to the limit. The poet Robert Southey reported that he saw a shaved monkey exhibited as a fairy.

Unfortunately, the fair also attracted wandering opportunists. Petty crime was rife. There was 'a plentiful supply of pickpockets, thieves, thimble riggers' (a sleight-of-hand con-artist game) 'and swindlers of every genus'.[36]

As time went by the commercial side of the fair dwindled while the drinking booths and entertainment increased. By the 1830s it was said to have become a centre of 'corruption and demoralisation'. A painting by Samuel Colman (1780-1845), in Bristol Museum and

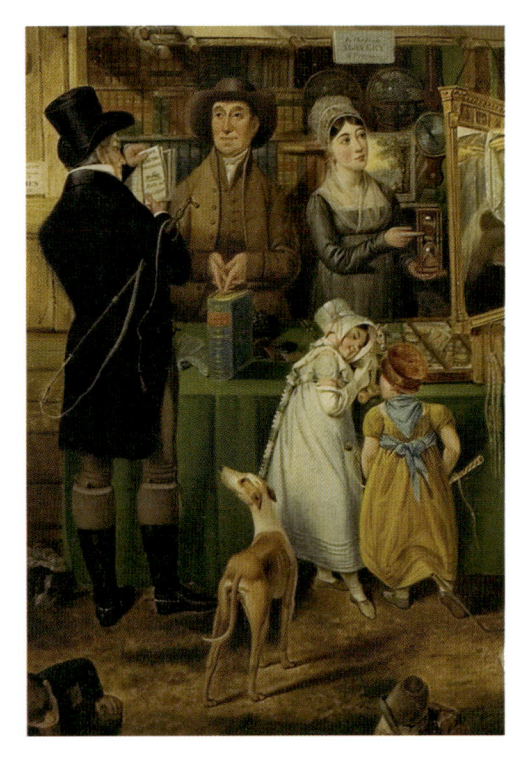

St James's Fair. Buying books and looking at fine cloth.

Art Gallery, depicts all the vice and virtue of St James's Fair. To the left are the pious shoppers buying books and looking at fine cloth; to the right a brothel, where a young girl is being enticed. In the background are rows of stalls and side shows along with swing boats, a big wheel and a menagerie featuring, if the poster is to be believed, a lion, an elephant, and a camel. All life is here: rich, poor, young, old.

St James's Fair, along with the smaller March Fair in Temple Street, was eventually abolished in 1838.[37]

ALL THE FUN OF THE FAIR

- Charles Heal and Sons -

The nature of fairs changed dramatically with the development of the steam engine. The pleasure fair offered steam powered roundabouts and ever-more exciting and sophisticated rides. Bristol's best-known showman was Charles Heal (1879-1950). Born in Glastonbury in 1879, by 1908 he was the proprietor of a splendid steam roundabout with galloping horses. Over the years he expanded his rides to include a helter-skelter, dodgems, a ghost ride and many other fairground favourites.

In 1935, the annual funfair on Durdham Down drew massive crowds. It was estimated 100,000 made the trek up Whiteladies Road. 'Amazing travel scenes were witnessed on tram, bus and train. Clifton Down Station disgorged well over 12,000 passengers...'[38]

From the 1930s to early 1970s Charles Heal's travelling fair's winter base was at the Batch in St Philips, just off Midland Road. Held in a yard, it was particularly popular during the Second World War. Charles Heal spoke of American GIs who would fling themselves off high-speed rides in the hope of breaking

Charles Heal's *Gallopers*. St George's Park Fair c.1944.
Reproduced with permission of the University of Sheffield.

an arm or a leg, so that they would be unable to fight. In November 1941, the fair was hit by a bomb and the dodgems and other rides destroyed. Replacement rides were swiftly brought in. One of Heal's associates at this time was the famous holiday camp impresario, Billy Butlin (1889-1980).

Around the corner, in Gloucester Lane, Old Market, was an area of waste land that was used for the travelling show people's winter quarters from the 1950s until the 1980s. The land is now a car park opposite the Coach and Horses. There was also a showmen's winter quarters in Lock's Yard, Bedminster.

Charles Heal's sumptuous living wagon is on display at the Fairground Heritage Centre, Lifton, Devon. PL16 0AT.

CHARLES HEAL & SONS
Bring the Greatest Show ever
THE
MOON ROCKET
GREATEST CARNIVAL THRILL

Electric Speedway, Noah's Ark, Startling Shows, Roundabouts, and all the Fun of the Fair

ROLL UP AND BE MERRY

WHAT'S IN A NAME?

- Six brands named after the city -

With a population of 436,000 Bristol is not a big city – but on the world stage it punches well above its own weight.

Being a port the name of Bristol has spread across the globe. When settlers moved to North America in the seventeenth and eighteenth centuries they liked to take a little bit of Bristol with them. There are said to be 35 populated places called Bristol across the world – the majority of them in Canada and the United States. *Hotel Bristol* also offers a welcoming bed in a surprising number of countries. There are at least 200 *Bristol* hotels, spread across Europe, Asia and the Americas. The origins of these hotels are unclear. They are not a chain. But they demonstrate the power of the name Bristol.

Bristol is proudly provincial – the capital of the South West. Traditionally, the city has looked outwards, not to London, but to the horizon and beyond. Independent and indomitable, Bristolians are adventurous, creative and enquiring. And sometimes irreverent; anarchic even. Think of the artist Banksy: once an outlaw, now a hero.

In the twenty-first century, there is a strong and ever-growing Bristol iconography. Clifton Suspension Bridge, Concorde, Cameron Balloons, Wallace and Gromit, pirates, Long John Silver and cider all consistently feature as representational images.

Bristolians are rightly proud of their city. So are Bristol businesses. Put 'Bristol' in your name and bask in the city's stardust.

The Bristol scroll

The Bristol scroll was first used by the British & Colonial Aeroplane Company in around 1910. Bristol planes, trams and buses continued to display the scroll continuously for around 80 years. In relatively recent times, other Bristol businesses adopted the design in company and product names including Smiles Brewery and Bristol Boats. Bristol Books has also adopted the 'B' for its company logo. The scroll lives on!

- Bristol Cars -

One of the initiatives at the end of the Second World War to maintain employment at Bristol Aeroplane Company (BAC) was the development of a car. The Bristol Car Company was intended to utilise the skills and expertise of an under-employed workforce. The first cars, produced in 1946, bore a startling resemblance to cars manufactured by BMW before the Second World War. How come? Legend has it blueprints from the bombed BMW factory in Germany were 'liberated' and sent back to the nascent motor engineers in Bristol.[39] The more plausible explanation for this uncanny similarity is that a franchise deal was signed with BMW.

Whatever the truth, the production of cars was always small, limited to an annual output of 150. Superbly designed, access to BAC's wind tunnel facilities meant their features were outstandingly streamlined.

The Bristol Car Company went into administration in 2011, but was subsequently bought by a private owner. One hundred people continued to work for the company, which was to produce 150 cars a year. The only place you could buy a new *Bristol* was through its show rooms in Kensington High Street. The latest version, the pleasingly retro *Bristol Bullet*, was to cost the price of a house.

But the respite was short-lived. Again, in May 2020, Bristol Car Company went into liquidation. Sadly, the *Bristol Bullet* never came on the market.

A Bristol Type 401 parked at the western end of the Suspension Bridge in this 1950s publicity shot.

Note the number plate. Type 401 was promoting itself again, this time in the City Centre.

Bristol Car Names
The Bristol Car Company branded their cars with some heavy-duty names.
- Beaufighter
- Brigand
- Brittania
- Blenheim
- Bullet
- Bristol Fighter

You knew you're buying something hard-core for your hundreds of thousands of pounds.

- Bristol Brabazon -

When it was first flown this massive eight-engine plane, built by the Bristol Aeroplane Company Ltd, was the biggest aircraft in the world. Filton runway had to be extended so that it could take-off and land. In the process the neighbouring village of Charlton was demolished.

The emphasis was on luxury. On board, there was a cocktail bar, a small cinema and private sleeping cabins. Built for the transatlantic routes, this supersized double-decker plane was designed to carry only 100 passengers. (In comparison, an Airbus Jumbo Jet A300 can typically take about

MAKING MONEY

Late 1940s and the *Brabazon* with its magnificent hangar in the background is nearing completion.

250 passengers.)

A technical success, but an economic disaster, the *Brabazon* never went into production. The order book remained empty; 'the queen of the skies' just wasn't financially viable. The future of air travel rested on economy rather than luxury. A flying ocean liner was too expensive and too slow. The project was cancelled in 1953.

Charlton village was destroyed for nothing. The enormous Brabazon hangars remain – at the time they were the largest hangars in the world – and 70 years later are being repurposed into an entertainment arena.

4 September, 1949 and the *Brabazon* returning to Filton on its maiden flight watched by around 10,000 people.

John Harvey Jnr overseeing the bottling of a special batch of magnum-sized *Bristol Cream* sherry to celebrate the Queen Elizabeth II's coronation in 1953.

- *Bristol Cream* -

Bristol has long had connections with the wine producing areas of Western Europe – Spain, France and Portugal. By the seventeenth century the city was famous for its own blend of sherry, *Bristol Milk*. A sweet sherry, so called, as it was the first moisture given to newborn babies in the city.[40] This was written in 1662.

In the 1860s, when the Denmark Street-based wine merchants Harveys were experimenting with a new blend of amontillado, the story goes that one of the tasters commented: 'if that's milk this must be the cream'. And so *Harveys Bristol Cream* was born.

In 1901, the Prince of Wales visited Bristol for the opening of Avonmouth Docks and was offered a glass of *Bristol Milk*. On tasting the drink he declared that 'the city must have some damn fine cows!'.

MAKING MONEY

Sherry tasters at work sampling another batch of *Bristol Cream* in the late 1930s.

A Bristol cellar man delivering a barrel of sherry.

- Bristol Cigarettes -

Bristol Cigarettes were one of the many brands of cigarette manufactured and licensed by W.D. & H.O. Wills. They were sold worldwide, especially in Commonwealth countries.

Wills's history dates back to 1786 when Henry Overton Wills joined Samuel Wilkinson in Castle Street. Initially, the majority of the tobacco was grown on the plantations of North America. Produced as pipe tobacco, it was sold under names such as *Bird's Eye*, *Honeydew* and the most popular brand, *Three Castles*.[41] Wills also made snuff and cigars.

Wills became part of the Imperial Tobacco Group in 1901. By that time it employed over 5,000 people in several factories spread across South Bristol.

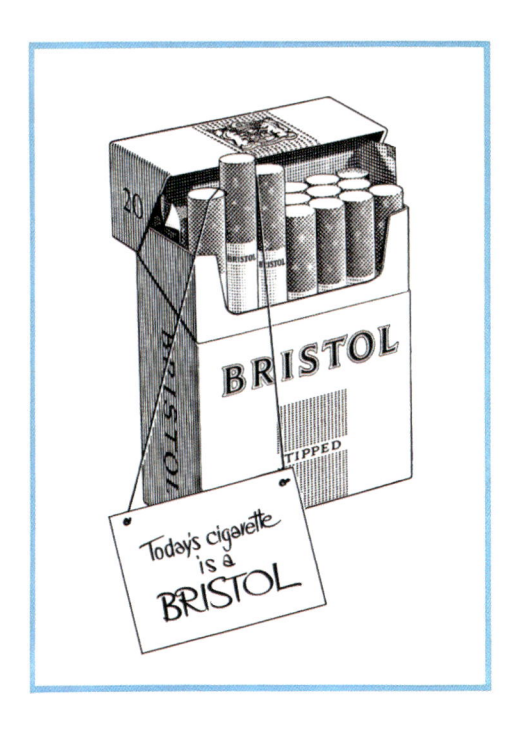

89

MANSON'S BRISTOL MISCELLANY

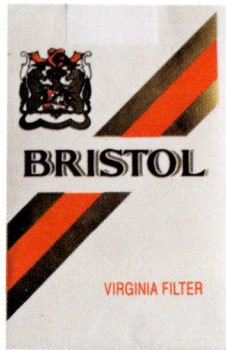

Bristol Cigarettes were one of the many brands of cigarette manufactured and licensed by W.D. & H.O. Wills.

Sorting cigarettes at one of the Bedminster factories.

It was during the First World War that mechanically-made cigarettes became widely popular. Those who survived the war came back addicted to nicotine.

Unmanufactured stocks of tobacco were stored in bonded warehouses. Initially, duty was only paid on tobacco when it was released for processing. Three of the substantial red brick warehouses still dominate the Ashton area of Bristol.

In the 1970s a new, state-of-the-art, factory was constructed at Hartcliffe. The warehouse was robotically controlled. It was so space-age that Dr Who and his sidekick were filmed on the roof, as well as running along the underground passageway that linked the factory to the offices.[42]

The Canon's Marsh bonded warehouses, made of reinforced concrete, were blown up in a controlled explosion one early Sunday morning in May 1988.[43] Lloyd's Bank administrative buildings and amphitheatre, overlooking the harbour, were built on the site.

The Hartcliffe factory was closed in 1990. The factory was demolished and is now the location of a retail park. The offices were converted to residential flats.

- Bristol Lodekka Bus -

The Bristol Tramways and Carriage Company Ltd built their first motor buses in 1908 in their Brislington tram depot. Four years later, motor bus production moved to a purpose built site a quarter of a mile away, just off Bath Road, Brislington. This is now the home of the Lodekka pub.

The famous *Lodekka* (get it?) bus was produced between 1953 and 1968. A revolutionary drive shaft configuration allowed the bus to be only 13 ft 6 inches high and therefore able to go under lower bridges.[44]

For a bus with a *Bristol* insignia on its radiator grill, it is surprising that the bodywork and seating was installed in Suffolk. The bare bus chassis's were driven across England to Lowestoft in all weathers by hardy drivers dressed like Second World War fighter pilots wrapped up in sheepskin bomber jackets and helmets.

The bus company was acquired, with a full order book, by British Leyland in 1982. In a financially incomprehensible move it was shut down a year later.

It was a *Lodekka* that Reg Varney drove in the 1970s TV comedy *On the Buses*. A *Lodekka* bus takes pride of place at Bristol Museum's M Shed.

A Bristol *Lodekka* at Broad Quay on its way to Portishead in the late 1960s. © Bristol Vintage Bus Group

- Bristol Blue Glass -

Not all Bristol glass is blue. In fact, coloured glass made up only a small proportion of output, the majority of production being for a more utilitarian use. The original *Bristol Blue Glass*, coloured by cobalt, was made by Issac Jacobs. At the beginning of the eighteenth century Jacobs produced exquisite tableware which was often gilded with classical motifs.

Bristol was well placed for production with its coal reserves and easy access to limestone, sand and lead – the main constituents of glass. Bristol's coal-fired glass industry came into its own in 1615 when it was forbidden to use wood – a dwindling resource – to fire glass furnaces.[45]

The manufacturing process took place in towering brick cones – some up to 30 metres high. The cityscape was littered with them. Some were not well built. In 1725, a cone collapsed when a storm hit the city, with a loss of 14 lives.[46] Later, 'a glass house belonging to Sir Abraham Elton Bart...suddenly fell down; happy it was for the glass men that the fire was out.'[47]

There were several types of glass made

in Bristol. Redcliffe sand was particularly good for the cheap brown glass used for bottling beer, cider, perry, wine and, of course, Hotwell Water. Fine clear window glass, called crown glass, was produced for the home and American market. Top of the range was flint glass which was used for the production of fine crystal goblets, decanters, sugar basins and other fashionable tableware.

In 1793, William Matthews, in his Bristol directory, recommended a visit to a glass works 'to satisfy their curiosity of observing these curious operations.' By 1797, 14 glassworks were in operation in Bristol.[48]

Unable to compete with the modern mass production methods of such firms as Pilkingtons, Bristol's last working glasshouse, Powell and Ricketts, of Redcliffe, closed in 1923.[49] The only physical remains of Bristol's once important glass industry are to be seen on Prewett Street, Redcliffe, where the base of a glass cone is used by the DoubleTree Hilton as a restaurant.

In 1988, Bristol Blue Glass Ltd was set-up to re-establish Bristol's long lost glass making skills. www.bristol-glass.co.uk.

At the beginning of the eighteenth century Issac Jacobs produced exquisite tableware which was often gilded with classical motifs. © Bristol Culture (Bristol Museum & Art Gallery).

ENDNOTES

1. Evans, J., *A Chronological Outline of the History of Bristol*, 1824, Bristol, p.46.
2. Sherborne. J.W., *The Port of Bristol in the Middle Ages*, 1971, Bristol Branch of the Historical Association, p.16.
3. ibid., p 16.
4. Harlow, J., *Traffic in Bristol Port in the later Seventeenth Century*. Talk to Avon Local History Association, 29 April 2019.
5. Defoe, D., *A Tour Through the Whole Island of Great Britain*, 1724-6, Penguin Edition 1978, p.362.
6. Sherborne J.W., op. cit., p. 5-6.
7. Walker D., *Bristol in the Early Middle Ages*, 1971, Bristol Branch of the Historical Association, p.7.
8. Platt, C., *The English Medieval Town*, 1979, Granada, p.105.
9. Lord, J. & Southam, J., *The Floating Harbour*, 1983, Redcliffe Press, p.9.
10. Sherborne J.W. op. cit., p.9.
11. ibid., p.17.
12. ibid., p.29.
13. Although Christopher Columbus first made landfall on a Caribbean Island in 1492, he only set foot on the American mainland in 1498.
14. Jones, E.T. & Condon, M.M., *Cabot and Bristol's Age of Discovery: The Bristol Discovery Voyages 1480-1509*, 2016, University of Bristol, p.40.
15. Witts, C., *Tales of the River Severn*, 1998, p.30.
16. Sherborne J.W., op. cit., p.29.
17. Sherborne, J., *William Canynges 1402-1474*. 1985, Bristol Branch of the Historical Association, p.8.
18. ibid., p.1.
19. *Adams's Chronicle of Bristol*, 1910, Arrowsmith, p.47.
20. Latimer, J. *The Annals of Bristol in the Eighteenth Century*, 1893, Bristol, p.88.
21. ibid., p.193.
22. *Adams's Chronicle of Bristol*, 1910, Arrowsmith, p.95.
23. Evans, J. *A Chronological Outline of the History of Bristol*, 1824, Bristol, p.226.
24. Defoe, D., *A Tour Through the Whole Island of Great Britain*, 1724-6, Penguin Edition 1978, p.363.
25. Wood, J. *A Description of the Exchange of Bristol*, 1745, Bath (Facsimile edition).
26. Dening, C.F.W., *Old Inns of Bristol*, 1943, Bristol, p.79.
27. Matthews, W., *A New History of Bristol or Complete Guide*, 1793, facsimile edition. p.42-5.
28. Latimer, J., *Annals of Nineteenth Century Bristol*, 1897, W. & F. Morgan, p.123.
29. *Arrowsmith's Dictionary of Bristol*, 1906, Arrowsmith, p.244-5.
30. Evans, J. *A Chronological Outline of the History of Bristol*, 1824, Bristol, p.93.
31. ibid., p.133.
32. *Adam's Chronicle of Bristol*, op. cit., p.112.
33. Sanger, 'Lord' G., *Seventy Years a Showman*, 1952, Dent, p.84.
34. Matthews, W., *A New History of Bristol or Complete Guide*,1794, facsimile edition. p.42.
35. Sanger, 'Lord' G., op. cit., p.40.
36. Latimer, J., *Annals of Nineteenth Century Bristol*, 1897, W. & F. Morgan. p.244.
37. ibid., p.123.
38. Belshaw, G. & Green, R., *Charles Heal and Son's Big Shows*, 2019, p.57.
39. Bolton, D., *Made in Bristol*, 2011, Redcliffe Press, p.38.
40. Fuller, T., *History of the Worthies of England, Vol. 2*, 1840, London. p.295.
41. Bristol Times and Mirror, *Work in Bristol*, 1883, p.85.
42. BBC TV *Dr Who*, Episode 95 - The Sun Makers (1977).
43. Jones, P. *Canon's Marsh - The Rise and Fall of the Tobacco Bonds*, 1988, Redcliffe Press, p.28.
44. ibid., p.32.
45. Witt,C., Weedon, C., and Schwind, A.P. *Bristol Glass*, Redcliffe Press, p.21.
46. ibid., p.23.
47. Witt,C., The Bristol Bottlemakers, 3 June 1978, Chemistry and Industry, p.379.
48. Latimer, J., *Annals of Eighteenth Century Bristol*, 1893, self published, p.486.
49. Witt,C., Weedon, C., and Schwind, A.P. op. cit., p.53.

BURDEN OF SHAME

ILL-GOTTEN GAINS

- The Triangular Trade -

It is an incontrovertible fact that much of Bristol's wealth in the eighteenth and early nineteenth centuries derived, directly or indirectly, from the triangular trade. The legacy of transatlantic slavery spreads far and wide and continues to haunt the city.

So what was the triangular trade? Put simply, ships laden with goods such as brass, jewellery, weapons and textiles left Bristol for the coast of West Africa. Here, this cargo was traded for kidnapped local people. These captured men and women were then forcibly shipped across the Atlantic to North America and the West Indies. Those who survived the passage were sold to estate owners to work on the sugar and tobacco plantations. Primarily sugar but also rum and tobacco were then shipped back to Bristol.[1] The barbarity of such an enterprise, a 'transatlantic disruption to humanity'[2], is almost too horrendous to countenance.

At each stage of the triangular trade there was money to be made. If all went according to plan, immense fortunes could be amassed.

Elmina Castle, Cape Coast, Ghana. From here, captured men and women were forcibly shipped across the Atlantic to North America and the West Indies.

In Bristol, over 160 years, thousands of people were involved in the slave economy. For example, as ship-owners, bankers, mortgage lenders to plantation owners, sugar merchants, sugar brokers and manufacturers of goods such as brass, glass and pottery.

It is estimated that between 1698 and 1807 over half a million Africans were transported by Bristol slave ships to the Caribbean.[3]

It is estimated that between 1698 and 1807 over half a million Africans were transported by Bristol slave ships to the Caribbean. © Bristol Culture (Bristol Museum & Art Gallery).

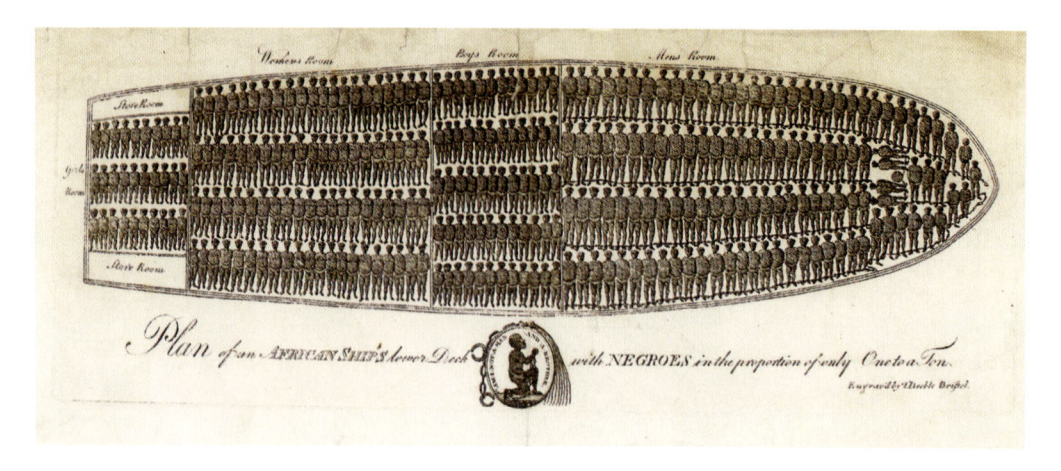

The British slave trade was made illegal in 1807. In some ways it was an empty victory. The outlawing of the trade meant nothing to the already enslaved people held on the plantations. Slavery remained central to Bristol's economy. The emancipation of enslaved peoples in British colonies did not take place until 1833. And even then the 'freed' were forced to labour for several years as unpaid sham 'apprentices'.

The number of enslaved people that were held in Bristol is open to debate. The Somerset judgement of 1772 stated that slaveholding was not allowed in England.[4] There were, however, a number of African slave-servants in the city. For some their status was little better than that of a slave. Newspaper adverts offered rewards for the capture of slaves who had fled their employers.[5] In Henbury churchyard an elaborate and grimly instructive tombstone to an 18-year-old 'negro servant' Scipio Africanus says it all:

I was born a PAGAN and a slave
Now sweetly sleep a CHRISTIAN in my grave.

Better a dead Christian than a live 'pagan'.

The eponymous Pero Jones (d.1798), one of nine children brought to Bristol from Nevis by John Pinney (1740-1818), was an enslaved-servant in the Pinney household in Great George Street.

One of Bristol's most infamous slave traders was Edward Colston (1636-1721). Colston was born in Temple Street but moved to London where he was a member of the Royal African Company, which had a monopoly on the British slave trade. During his time at the Royal African Company 85,000 enslaved African men, women and children were purchased, branded and forced onto their ships. Colston's investment in this evil enterprise made him a multi-millionaire in today's terms. He never forgot his home town and endowed schools and charities through his ill-gotten gains.

When slavery was eventually abolished it was the plantation owners, NOT the enslaved, who were given £20million recompense. In Bristol just under 100 people, over a quarter of whom were women, received approximately £411,000 in compensation for more than 25,000 enslaved people.'[6] According to the Legacies of British Slave-ownership Database, Charles Pinney, of 7 Great George Street (now the Georgian House Museum), received

BURDEN OF SHAME

£12,515 compensation for his 1,328 slaves on 11 plantations across the Caribbean.

These dubious payouts were used to invest in a range of enterprises that would stimulate the economy. Many awardees invested in the Great Western Railway. It is likely that the Great Western Cotton Factory in Barton Hill would not have been built without compensation money.

There is a growing feeling that a significant memorial or commemoration is required to enable reconciliation. The Victorians re-invented Colston as a merchant prince and moral saint – naming the new concert hall after him in 1867 and in 1895 erecting his statue in the Centre. Knowing what we know now these

In Henbury churchyard there is an elaborate and grimly instructive tombstone to the 18-year-old Scipio Africanus.

memorials are a misguided embarrassment. During a Black Lives Matter demonstration in June 2020 Colston's celebratory statue was pulled down and unceremoniously thrown into the docks.

The hard facts of this shameful period need to be stated sensitively and thoughtfully. Until this difficult aspect of Bristol's past is aired and understood it will be difficult for the healing to begin. As Bob Marley sang, 'If you know your history then you would know where you coming from.'[7]

Colston's celebratory statue in central Bristol was pulled down in June 2020 during a Black Lives Matters demonstration and thrown unceremoniously into the docks.

Africans in Bristol

The history of black people in Bristol is not just about plantations in the Americas. There is evidence of Africans living in the city since the time of Elizabeth I. Bristol as a port had international links; it seems likely that Africans visited and even settled in the city. Church records for the central parishes list scores of 'negros' and 'blacks' being baptised, married and buried during the eighteenth century.[8]

An inventory of the personal possessions of an African woman, Cattelena, made after her death in 1625, lists bedding, pots and pans, boxes and, most significant of all, a cow.[9] Her goods, valued at £6 9s 6d were valuable enough to be listed by the authorities. How she got them we do not know. Perhaps she was left them by a previous employer? The cow was a sure sign that Cattelena, who lived to the north of Bristol in Almondsbury, had some degree of independence.

Links with Bristol were so important that the Americans established their first consulate in Europe in Queen Square in 1792.

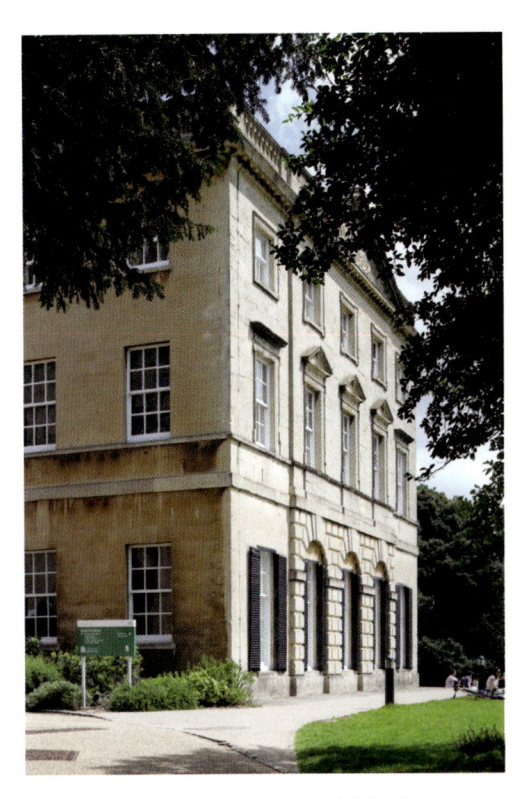

Royal Fort, Tyndall's Park. The Tyndall family were bankers to the slave trade and had part shares in slaving ships.

Many of Bristol's grand houses have slavery connections.
- **Blaise Castle House**. Residence of Thomas Farr, slave ship owner and sugar merchant.
- **Cornwallis House**, Clifton. Home of the Hobhouse family, who had widespread investments in slaving ships.
- **Georgian House**, 7, Great George Street. The Pinney family had sugar plantations on the Caribbean island of Nevis.
- **Goldney House**, Clifton. The Goldney family exported metal goods to the West African coast.
- **Leigh Court**, Leigh Woods. Home of the Miles family, connected with plantations in Jamaica and Trinidad. After 1833, **Kings Weston House** became the Miles's family seat.
- **Royal Fort**, Tyndall's Park. The Tyndall family were bankers to the slave trade and had part shares in slaving ships.

- American Consulate -

Links with Bristol were so important that the Americans established their first consulate in Europe in Queen Square in 1792. Bristol continued to trade with both the northern and southern States after American Independence in 1774. Exports of largely slave-produced tobacco featured prominently in Bristol's economy.[10]

ENDNOTES

1. Dresser, M. & Giles, S. *Bristol and Transatlantic Slavery*, 1999, Bristol Museums and Art Gallery, p.10.
2. Phrase used by Ros Martin during a talk *Colston: Fact or Fiction* at the Bristol Festival of Literature, 19 October 2020.
3. Slave Voyages Database. https://www.slavevoyages.org/ I am indebted to Ruth Hecht and Roger Ball for this information.
4. Blackburn, R., *The Overthrow of Colonial Slavery 1776 -1848*, 1988, Verso, p.99-101.
5. Dresser, M. & Giles, S., op. cit. p.121-2.
6. Legacies of Slave Ownership database. https://www.ucl.ac.uk/lbs/person/view/45909. I am indebted to Ruth Hecht and Roger Ball for the provision of these figures.
7. Bob Marley, Buffalo Soldier, 1983.
8. Lindegaard, D.P., *Black Bristolians of the 18th and 19th Centuries*, self-published, 1990s?
9. Kaufman, M., *Black Tudors*, 2017, One World, p. 250.
10. Dresser, M., Jordan, C. & Taylor, D., *Slave Trade Trail*, Bristol Museums and Art Gallery, 1998, p.10.

BRISTOL'S SWANSONG

AN INADEQUATE AND OLD FASHIONED HARBOUR

- Building the Floating Harbour[1] -

The first national census of England in 1801 judged Bristol's population to be a mere 65,000. This was much lower than the previously supposed 100,000. The census proved what many well-travelled people had already observed: that Bristol had slipped well behind its rival Liverpool as holder of the cherished position of second city in the nation. Trade had been adversely affected by the American War of Independence. Bristol was also precariously dependent on imports from the West Indies.[2]

Bristol's decline was further hastened by the condition of its inadequate and old-fashioned harbour. Only with great difficulty could the docks handle the large ocean-going ships that now plied the Atlantic. For many years efforts had been made to improve the shipping accommodation offered by the port; plans had first been drawn up in 1765. But it was not until the full implications of the census had sunk in that the matter was considered seriously.

One of the main objectives of designs drawn up by William Jessop (1745-1814) was to remove the inconvenience caused by the ebb and flow of the tide. Jessop's plan was to dig a new channel for the Avon – the Avon New Cut – while converting, with the aid of locks and dams, the original course of the river into a two-and-a-half mile floating harbour.

The main entrance into the float was to be through the Cumberland Basin lock gates. At high tide, smaller vessels would also be able to sail up the Cut and enter through a side entrance into the triangular Bathurst Basin which would cover the site of the former Treen Mills pond, fed by the Malago Brook. There was a further lock entrance at Temple Meads.

Jessop's design was not original. In fact, it echoed suspiciously a similar proposal put forward in 1791 by the vicar of Temple Church, the Reverend William Milton. The Dock Company was reluctant to admit this, and only

The main entrance into the float was through the Cumberland Basin lock gates. Watercolour by Samuel Jackson, c.1825. © Bristol Culture (Bristol Museum & Art Gallery).

grudgingly did they acknowledge that their concept owed anything to Milton's original inspiration. As a sop they did, however, award the Reverend with 'a piece of plate not exceeding the value of one hundred guineas'.[3]

The building of the Floating Harbour was an undertaking that demanded a large labour force. Six hundred navvies started work in 1804. But by the end of the project their numbers had swollen to over 1,000. Regardless of a long standing tradition that the Cut was dug by French prisoners, there are, in fact, no records to verify this.

The digging of the Cut was an astounding sight. The earth was removed down to the bare red sandstone rock. The rock was then blasted by explosives. The rubble was put into carts and pulled out of the excavation by new-fangled steam-powered engines.[4]

The building of the Cut also required the construction of two iron bridges: one to the south of Redcliffe Hill (Bedminster Bridge), the other at the bottom of Pylle Hill, in the fields of Temple Meads (Harford Bridge).

Progress was slow. It soon became clear that the cost and length of the task had been seriously under-estimated. In the end the works took over a year longer, and cost twice as much, as originally planned. At last, on 1 May, precisely five years after its inauguration, the Docks Company was proud, and somewhat relieved, to announce that:

'after struggling through numberless unforeseen difficulties . . . after having perhaps undertaken to perform in a given time more than it appears possible in the capacity of human art to execute, the directors of this concern have fulfilled their engagement.' [5]

The construction of the Floating Harbour had finally been completed. To celebrate the event the directors of the Dock Company treated the labourers to a dinner. *Felix Farley's Bristol Journal* cheerfully reported: 'In the good old style of English hospitality, `two whole oxen, 6 cwt of plumb pudding, 1,000 gallons

At high tide, smaller vessels would sail up the Cut and enter through a side entrance into the Bathurst Basin.
© Bristol Culture (Bristol Museum & Art Gallery).

of stingo and other things in proportion had been provided'.

But as the stingo was consumed, emotions rose. The *Journal* carried on to say that 'the people indulged themselves of all the graceful eccentricities of liberty'.

However, 'upon the arrival of a cart with a fresh supply of ale, some honest Hibernians proceeded rather unceremoniously to disburden the vehicle of its contents'.

The sight of the sack of the beer wagon was just too much for the patience of the John Bulls and soon a full scale drunken brawl broke out. The dinner, now turned riot, was only terminated by the interference of the police and the press gang. Several of the labourers spent the night sobering up in gaol.[6]

The Floating Harbour was a grand undertaking and even today it is an epic monument to the spirit of nineteenth century Bristol. It is still virtually intact and now represents the very heart and character of the city. The Floating Harbour also encouraged the expansion of shipbuilding. Two of the first ocean-going steamships, Brunel's, *Great Western* (1837) and *Great Britain* (1843) were built alongside the floating harbour and inched through its almost too-small locks.

Even so, this show of confidence was not enough to halt the downward turn in trade. Unfortunately, the Bristol Dock Company sought to recover its investment by imposing unrealistic port charges which only served to send business elsewhere, particularly to arch-rival Liverpool.[7]

And there was still the problem of ever-larger ships negotiating the twisting, tidal Avon. Vessels would regularly run aground. Some would break their backs, blocking the river for days. One of the worst accidents occurred in 1851 when the newly built *S.S. Demerara*, second only in size to the *S.S. Great Britain*, hit a mud bank during its inaugural journey down the Avon. The stern consequently swung round and became firmly lodged on the

If ships had trouble coming up to Bristol's docks, the answer was to move the docks further downstream. Avonmouth Dock opened 1877; Portishead 1879.

opposite side of the river. As the tide ebbed the boat began to crack in the middle. The ship was an insurance write-off before it had even reached the sea.[89]

The answer was obvious. If ships have trouble coming up to the docks, move the docks further downstream. Thus new modern docks opened at Avonmouth in 1877 and on the other side of the river at Portishead in 1879. Both were linked to a wider railway network.

In reality the building of the Floating Harbour had turned out to be the port's swansong.

Bathurst Basin

Bathhurst Basin is built on the site of the old Treen Mills pond. The mill pond was created by damming the Malago Stream before it flowed into the Avon. It was a favourite haunt for duck hunting.

The Bathust Basin, named after Bristol's M.P. Sir Charles Bathurst (1754-1831), served as a side entrance to the docks. Smaller vessels could sail up the Cut and enter the harbour by the Bathurst Basin lock.

The lock was filled in during the Second World War, when it was feared that damage from bombs could lead to the sudden emptying of water from the harbour.

ENDNOTES

1   A longer version of this article of appeared in Manson, M., *Bristol Beyond the Bridge*, 1988, Redcliffe Press, p. 69-71.
2   Malpass, P., *The Bristol Dock Company, 1803 -1848*, 2010, ALHA Booklet, p.4.
3   Malpass, P. & King, A. *Bristol's Floating Harbour: The First 200 Years*, 2009, Redcliffe, p.29.
4   White, K. & Gallop, R., *A Celebration of the Avon New Cut*, 2006, Fiducia Press, p.13-4.
5   *Felix Farley's Bristol Journal* 29 April 1809.
6   *Felix Farley's Bristol Journal* 13 May 1809.
7   Harvey, C. & Press, J., Ed, *Studies in the Business History of Bristol*, 1988, Bristol Academic Press, p.5.
8   The Demerara was, in fact, repaired and later re-launched as *The British Empire*. https://www.brh.org.uk/site/articles/wrecks-on-the-river-avon/
9   Latimer, J. *Annals of Nineteenth Century Bristol*, 1897, W. & F. Morgan. p.328.

'JOLLY COLLIERS'

A ONCE IMPORTANT INDUSTRY
- Coal -

These days it's difficult to believe that Bristol was once celebrated for its coal fields. The clanking pit heads and ugly slag heaps have long gone. Apart from the occasional sudden and unwelcome appearance of a gaping hole in a garden, or the collapse of a road, today there is little evidence of this once important industry.

Despite being of low quality and the seams thin, coal played a major role in Bristol's economic development in the seventeenth, eighteenth and nineteenth centuries. Daniel Defoe reported in 1724 'tis very remarkable, that the city is so plentifully supplied with coals'. At its peak in the 1890s around 3,500 were employed in coal mining in Bristol.

> **Extent of the coal field:**
> '... extending from Cromall in the north to the slopes of the Mendip Hills in the south, a distance of some 26 miles, and from the neighbourhood of Bath in the east to Nailsea in the west, about 24 miles.'
> *Bristol and Somerset Coalfield Regional Survey Report.*

Disregarding the pub's name, the collier's life was far from jolly. The coal was dug with pickaxe and shovel. It was lung-busting, back-breaking and knee-wrecking work. Some of the seams were barely four feet high so the day would be spent on hands and knees. The miner dug the coal; the collier brought the coal up from the coal-face.[1]

Coalpit Heath Colliery between the first and second world wars. © Bristol Culture (Bristol Museum & Art Gallery).

A coal pit in Long Ashton c.1790. Shows pit buildings and colliers collecting and selling coal. Thomas Bonnor
© Bristol Culture (Bristol Museum & Art Gallery).

The earliest mines were merely holes dug in the ground or shallow pits called 'bell pits'. Hence the name Coalpit Heath. Miners would dig down and then outwards until the pits were teetering on collapse. It was a dangerous business.

With the invention of the steam engine more extensive mining became possible. Steam engines were used for pumping water out of the mines as well as powering the hoisting equipment. Pit ponies pulled the coal wagons. In 1875, at 1,800 feet, Malago Vale was the deepest pit. Mining could occur as much as two miles away from the shaft. Some mines interconnected: the Whitehall Colliery was linked to the Easton colliery.

Health and safety considerations were minimal. Miners working on the rock face could be as young as 14-years-old[2] – though there are tales of boys as young as ten, working in pitch darkness, looking after the doors that controlled the ventilation.[3]

Although Bristol mines were classified as 'non fiery', explosions did occur. In 1886, at Dean Lane Pit, eight men were killed instantly in an explosion.[4] In Malago Pit, in 1891, at least ten men died in a blast.[5]

The most common cause of injury and death was rock fall. In 1851, 50 colliers were trapped in a Bedminster pit. Eventually, volunteer rescuers got through to the confined men and after being in the pit for 40 hours they were all brought alive to the surface.[6]

The Davy Safety Lamp, invented in 1815 by Humphrey Davy, was a life-saver. The lamp could indicate by the flame dimming and burning blue instead of yellow whether there

'JOLLY COLLIERS'

Frog Lane Pit, Coalpit Heath in around 1906. First sunk in 1853, the pit employed 258 miners until closed by the National Coal Board in 1949.

Speedwell Pit in around 1890. The last fatal accident in a Bristol coal mine happened here in 1932 when Jack Emery, colliery firemen died during the rescue of two colleagues. The Pit closed in 1936 with the loss of 310 miners jobs.

Deep Pit in around 1890. Along with Speedwell, it formed the Kingswood Colliery. It operated from the late eighteenth century until closure in 1936.

Parkfield Colliery, Pucklechurch in around 1890. Sunk in 1851, the coal seams were reached two years later. With flooding increasing pumping costs it, too, closed in 1936.

Easton Colliery, 1900. Closed 1911. The site of the former colliery is now Felix Road adventure playground. In 1886 an explosion killed eight miners. © Bristol Culture (Bristol Museum & Art Gallery).

was a build up of gas. Even so, candles were the usual means of lighting. Davey lamps were often only issued once there had been an explosion. Too late for some.

Explosions could also be caused by fine coal dust hanging in the air.[7] A coal dust explosion happened in Dean Lane Colliery in 1889. The ventilation system was put out of action by the blast. Consequently, nine people died from suffocation.[8]

The miners were paid by the amount of coal they cut. Despite being strongly unionised the money was not high. But you could earn more working down the pit than on the factory floor at Wills's or Robinson's.[10] Miners received an allowance of free coal; they also received free medical attention from the pit doctor or the local hospitals.[11]

Even so, in comparison with other mining areas, the conditions in Bristol's pits were harsh. Experienced miners from South Wales and the Forest of Dean would only stay a couple of weeks or so as the conditions were too bad for them.

For those who held the mining rights it was another matter – fortunes were made. The Smyths, who owned land in Bedminster and Ashton, lived in imposing style on their Ashton Court Estate. Handel Cossham (1824-90) owner of collieries in Easton, St George and Kingswood, became a liberal MP (1885-90) for Bristol East and put money towards the establishment of St George's Park and the founding of Cossham Hospital – much used by injured miners.

By the beginning of the twentieth century Bristol coal became less profitable to mine. The seams were difficult to work and the quality of coal not as high as that from South Wales and other parts of Great Britain.

When the Dean Lane Pit, Southville, closed in 1906 the land was given by Dame Emily Smyth to the city for use as a park. A bandstand, long gone, was placed on the pit head.

In 1904 the following collieries were in operation:[9]
- Ashton Vale
- Coalpit Heath
- Dean Lane
- Easton
- Hanham
- Kingswood
- Parkfield,
- South Liberty, South Bristol.

Easton Colliery, Bristol, c.1900. Wagons are loaded with debris by two workers. Other details include the timber headstock and dram lines. The peak of production was in the 1870s.
© Bristol Culture (Bristol Museum & Art Gallery).

Closure of the Coalfields

- Malago Vale, Bedminster – closed 1897.
- Ashton Vale – closed 1906.
- Dean Lane, Bedminster – closed 1906.
- Shortwood Lodge, Mangotsfield – closed 1908.
- Whitehall Colliery and Easton Colliery – closed 1911.
- South Liberty, Bedminster – closed 1926.
- Deep Pit, St George – closed 1936.
- Parkfield – closed 1936.
- Speedwell Pit – closed 1936.
- Coalpit Heath – closed 1949.
- Harry Stoke – closed 1963.

The Somerset Coalfield continued in operation for a while longer. The last working mines, Writhlington and Kilmersdon, closed in 1973.

ENDNOTES

1. 'CLASS' *Miner's Memories*, 1984(?), Adult Studies Department, South Bristol Technical College, p.14.
2. Moss, F., *City Pit*, 1986, Bristol Broadsides, p.14.
3. 'CLASS', op. cit., p.6.
4. ibid., p.40.
5. ibid., p.43.
6. South Gloucestershire Mines Research Group, *Kingwood Coal*, 2008, p.23.
7. 'CLASS', op. cit., p.37.
8. South Gloucestershire Mines Research Group, *Kingwood Coal*, 2008, p.24.
9. *Arrowsmith's Dictionary of Bristol*, 1906, Arrowsmith, p.109-10.
10. 'CLASS' op. cit., p.33.
11. ibid., p.27.

SEIZED BY A SUDDEN DEATH

'THERE DIED IN A MANNER THE WHOLE STRENGTH OF THE TOWN'

- Plague -

The bubonic plague first appeared in England in 1348.

'This year, 1348, and the following there was a general mortality through the whole world…This grievous plague entered the maritime part of the country by Southampton and came to Bristol, and there died in a manner the whole strength of the town, seized as it were by a sudden death.'[1]

The Black Death, as the plague is more commonly known, killed between a third and a half of England's five to six million inhabitants. It took 200 years for the population to recover to its previous level. This dreadful disease, spread by fleas from black rats, was a haunting presence for over three centuries. Swift, virulent and incurable, nine out of ten of its victims died. It is said that a person could go to bed healthy and die the following day. In Bristol the population was so depleted that 'grass grew several inches high in High Street and Broad Street'.[2]

There were some unexpected social side-effects from the Black Death. For those who did survive it was a time of opportunity; there was a shortage of labour and, in spite of the King ordering otherwise, workers felt empowered to demand higher wages.

Over the following centuries the plague continued to raise its fearsome head. There were at least seven outbreaks in Bristol between 1361 and 1646. In 1574-5, 2,000 people died. In 1603, the toll was nearly 2,600.

Authorities were generally at a loss as to how to contain the illness. There was, however, the hazy concept of self-isolation and quarantine. Indeed, quarantine comes from the Italian for 40 days – the time infected sailors were expected to stay in isolation off-shore, which makes the two-week self-isolation period in 2020 for Covid-19 seem lightweight.

Contaminated households were boarded-up with the occupants incarcerated inside. The front door would be marked with a foot long red cross with the chilling inscription written above: 'Lord have mercy upon us.' The sale of clothes and bedding from an infected house was 'utterly prohibited', while burials were to be in the dark, 'before sun rising or after sun setting'.[3] Pitch and Pay Lane, Stoke Bishop, is said to have been named after a spot where farmers, during times of plague, would leave their goods for sale, thus avoiding potential contact with the infected.

Henry VIII was to visit Bristol in 1534 but, with the plague raging, he stayed at Thornbury Castle for ten days instead. In 1603, no one was allowed to attend St James's Fair from London unless they had a certificate from the Lord Mayor stating that they had not come from an infected house. In 1636, with the pestilence raging in the capital, London traders were banned altogether from the fair.[4]

Another mysterious malady was the so-called sweating sickness. In 1551, between Easter and Michaelmas (29 September) sweating sickness in Bristol 'swept away many hundreds a week'. The disease inexplicably faded away.

To add to the misery, in 1635, there was an outbreak of smallpox 'never by memory of man so fearful and infectious'.

During the outbreak of plague in 1638, goods were quarantined in the open fields of Tyndall's Park and a 'pest house' for those suffering from the disease was established on St Michael's Hill. This soon proved to be too small and temporary hovels were erected nearby.

In 1646, in St James's parish, 400 people died from the plague; in the healthier St Michael's 180 were struck down by the disease; in all 3,000 perished in Bristol.[5]

Although the plague mysteriously disappeared from the British Isles after 1665, there are still rare outbreaks in other parts of the world. These days, it can at least be treated by antibiotics.

Leprosy

A leper hospital, St Lawrence's, was established in 1208 outside Lawford's Gate – hence Lawrence Hill. In 1345 it was decreed that 'No leprous man was to stay within the precincts' (of Bristol).

A TREATMENT FOR 'HOT LIVERS, FEEBLE BRAINS AND RED PIMPLY FACES'

- The Hotwell -

The first reference to a warm spring was made by William Worcester in 1480, who mentioned a spring a 'bow shot away' from the Avon Gorge that was 'as warm as milk or the water at Bath'.[6] More warm than hot, the water sprang out of the rock at a constant 76° Fahrenheit. Like the waters from Bath, it was believed that anything that tasted so awful must do you good.

Although there were a number of springs issuing from the rocks of the Avon Gorge, the one that was thought to be the most efficacious was in a particularly inconvenient position. The slightly gaseous water issued through the mud 10 feet above low water level.[7] In 1696, to prevent the fresh water from becoming contaminated, Hotwell House was built around and above it. Hotwell House, which jutted out over the river, provided a pump room with spectacular views – if, at low tide, you ignored the mud and slime – of ships coming up and down the river

The range of ailments thought to be cured by drinking Hotwell water increased over the years. In 1650 it was recommended for 'hot livers, feeble brains and red pimply faces'.[8] By 1680 it was promoted by local physicians as a treatment for diabetes, and then, later, for tuberculosis.

Daniel Defoe observed in 1724 that Hotwell water was bottled and sent all over the world. It also, he noted, made very good tea.

The cure, which required the consumption of six half-pint glasses of the warm water per day, required patience. Alexander Pope noted that a six-to-eight week stay was required as the waters compared to those of Bath 'were of no great strength'.[9] One lady reported that 'after five years she now continues well'.[10] One wonders if, perhaps, it was merely a matter of letting the malady take its course.

In between sipping the waters the invalids could ride on the Downs, catch a pleasure boat to Portishead or take the Rownham Meads ferry for a gentle ramble to the 'sweet and wholesome' village of Ashton, where a cream tea could be purchased.

The social events offered by a spa were as much a part of the cure as the water. During the season, which lasted from April to September, musicians played in the pump room every morning. Yet the Bristol Hotwell was never going to rival the gay society of Bath. Bristol was a city of trade, industry and hard work. By the end of the eighteenth century visitors to the Hotwell had dwindled to a small number of discouraging patients. The water was expensive and the social contacts disappointing.

In 1820 Hotwell House was demolished to make way for what would later become Bridge Valley Road.

Today, on a cold winter's morning, if you look over the river wall opposite the abandoned Clifton Rocks Railway, it is said that a thin mist from the warm stream can still be spotted rising out of the mud at low tide.

MANSON'S BRISTOL MISCELLANY

LAUGHTER IS THE BEST MEDICINE
- A cure for consumption? -

The history of medicine is littered with bizarre apparatus, bitter pills and strong doses of quackery.

In 1798, the Shropshire-born Dr Thomas Beddoes (1760-1808) moved his Bristol Pneumatic Institute to Dowry Square, Hotwells.[11] The Pneumatic Institute was established for the treatment, by inhalation, of consumption (tuberculosis). Beddoes's approach was experimental to say the least. His claim to fame was the use of nitrous oxide – laughing gas! Even if the gas didn't cure the lung condition, at least patients died laughing.

The apparatus for the production of the gas, and the mechanism for its inhalation, was constructed by the celebrated steam engineer, James Watt (1736-1819).

Beddoes was assisted in his experiments by the young Humphrey Davy (1778-1829) who had moved to Bristol from Penzance. The poets Samuel Taylor Coleridge (1772-1834) and Robert Southey (1774-1843), both close friends of Beddoes, were enthusiastic guinea pigs. The future Poet Laureate Southey, clearly still in a state of euphoria, wrote to his brother Tom:

'Oh Tom! Such gas has Davy discovered, the gaseous oxide! Oh Tom! I have had some; it made me laugh and tingly in every toe and finger tip. Davy has actually invented a new pleasure, for which language has no name. Oh Tom! I am going for more this evening; it makes one strong and so happy! So gloriously happy!...Oh excellent airbag! Tom, I am sure the air in heaven must be this wonder working air of delight'.[12]

Dowry Square, Hotwells. Home of the Bristol Pneumatic Institute.

There was a serious side to all this hilarity. Beddoes's and Davy's experiments paved the way for the application of anaesthetics.

The precocious Davy was soon appointed as an Assistant Lecturer in Chemistry at the Royal Institution in London.

Davy is best remembered for the invention of the Miner's Safety Lamp. The cylindrical lamp was surrounded by gauze which protected the flame from igniting fire damp. A change in the colour of the flame would warn the miner of the presence dangerous gases. The lamp saved many lives. Davy was Knighted in 1812 and made a Baronet in 1818.[13]

After Davy's departure, business at the Pneumatic Institute slowed. The Institute closed in 1801.

ENDNOTES

1. Seyer, S., *Memoirs Historical and Topographical of Bristol*, 1823, Bristol. p.144.
2. ibid., p.143.
3. The Newes, Numb 52, July 6 1665. B.R.O 12781/4.
4. Latimer, J., *Annals of the Seventeenth Century*, 1900, Bristol, p.137.
5. A Fellow of the Queen's College Oxford. *The Sieges of Bristol.* 1868. Bristol. p.38.
6. Matthews, W., *Complete Guide and Bristol Directory*. Bristol 1793 (Facsimile edition), p.98.
7. ibid., p.98.
8. Waite, V., *The Bristol Hotwell* in *Bristol in The Eighteenth Century*. 1972, David and Charles, p.114.
9. Bettey, J.H.. *Bristol Observed*. 1989, Redcliffe, p.68.
10. Waite, V., op. cit., p.118.
11. Latimer, J., *The Annals of Bristol in the Eighteenth Century*, 1893, Bristol, p.503.
12. Hutton, S., *Bristol and its Famous Associations*, 1907, Bristol, p.275.
13. Fedden, M., *Bristol Bypaths*. 1955, Bristol (?), p.42-5.

PUBLIC HEALTH

'...THE FILTH AND STENCH WERE ALMOST INTOLERABLE'

- Privys, cess pits and sewers -

In 1831, there was a cholera outbreak in the older, more crowded and unsanitary parts of the city. Of the 1,500 cases reported, one third ended in death. Although a firm link between clean water and good health had not yet been fully established, there was a strong suspicion that cholera was linked to the consumption of tainted drinking water.

While the precise science wasn't known, it was observed that there was a connection between lack of drainage and certain diseases. Before the invention of the flushable water closet, the universal toilet was the privy – basically, a plank of wood with a cess pit below. In most houses the privy was in the back-yard. In courts and alleyways they would be shared with neighbours. Every so often, it could be years, the cess pit would be emptied by the 'night soil men', so called as this tricky task was traditionally done under the cover of darkness. The contents were carried away to be spread on nearby market gardens or dumped at the nearest convenient spot. It was a hazardous practice as the untreated 'soil' may well have contained disease-causing pathogens.

There was no overall city plan and sewage was disposed of in exactly the same way as it had been for centuries. In Bristol's early days the tidal range of the Avon offered a great advantage, draining even the lowest areas. But over time, as the population grew, the city expanded beyond the reach of this natural cleansing system. During the drier summer months Bristol's smaller brooks would turn into putrefying cess pits. In Bedminster, 'a poor, dirty, unventilated district', there were virtually no sewers at all, and very few in St Jude's and St Philip's.[1] Frequently, the construction of sewers was woefully inadequate, leading to leaks and the contamination of sources of drinking water.

The lack of clean water and effective sewers was replicated in cities across the country. The Government was so concerned

One room, slum housing in the shadow of St Mary Redcliffe Church. © Bristol Culture (Bristol Museum & Art Gallery).

about the increasing outbreaks of disease in the rapidly growing urban areas that, in 1845, they commissioned a number of reports into the public health of towns. In the account written by Sir Henry de la Beche, Bristol did not come out well. The mortality rate in the city was said to be scandalously high, exceeded only by the notoriously unhealthy conurbations of Manchester and Liverpool.[2]

Unsurprisingly, a cholera epidemic struck again in 1849, killing 444 people in Bristol.

It was noted at an emergency meeting of local doctors in Orchard Street that the disease came 'from the atmosphere'. Cholera was particularly associated with houses that had bad drainage, had 'back to back' courts, were filthy or had limited water supply.[3] 'Look at Bedminster with its open ditch poisoning the atmosphere and spreading disease and death around'. It wouldn't be until 1854 that the cholera bacillus was finally identified.

So what could be done to improve public health in the Bristol? The City Council had only basic powers to deal with insanitary nuisances. The Public Health Act of 1848 had already established a National Board of Health with enforcement powers. Subsequently, Superintending Inspector G.T. Clark (1808-98) was invited to Bristol to investigate.[4]

Clark, a polymath who had trained as a surgeon, worked as an engineer under I.K. Brunel and inherited an iron works in Wales, embraced his task enthusiastically. His 1850 report paints in detail a squalid city teetering on the brink of disaster. As he conducted his examination the inspector wrote, 'at times, the filth and stench were almost intolerable'.

Clark found ramshackle, overcrowded, unventilated courts and alleyways. 'In the old city many of the streets are tortuous, narrow and encumbered with ancient houses, much admired by those who do not live in them. They are mostly crazy, lodging five or six families in accommodations intended for one'.[5]

The paradox is that while Victorian Britain was the wealthiest country in the world much of its population faced appalling living conditions. The inhabitants of Bristol had more than doubled to 137,000 during the first half of the nineteenth century.[6] The provision of housing for this fast growing and mobile population was unsustainable. Clark found rooms quite unfit for human habitation let to whole families. 'There are two beds in the room, which contains a family of ten persons.' Even an under pavement coal-hole was used as a bedroom.

In an age of horse-drawn transport manure was everywhere. As was waste and offal from slaughterhouses. In the centre of the city there were piggeries and stables while the Fish Market next to St Nicholas Church was reported to be in a dirty condition. There were seven abattoirs in St Paul's and three in St James's. Tellingly, off Old Market, there was a street named Dead Horse Lane (now Waterloo Street). It was also known, perhaps ironically, as Lucky Lane.

Privies were placed near water pumps; there were half-hearted drains with offensive stenches. Latrines were emptied of 'night soil' and their contents deposited directly into the Frome or the Avon. The Frome was hardly recognisable as a river anymore. The Law Ditch, an open sewer that drained Redcliffe,

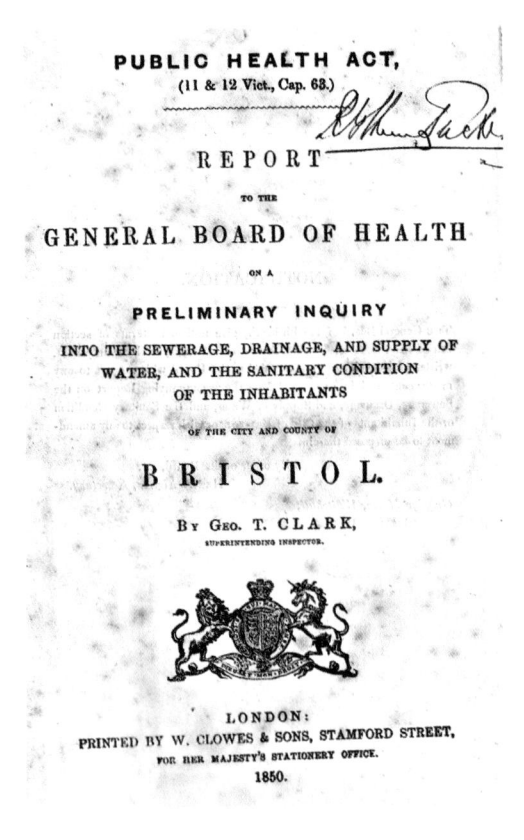

Clark's 1850 report into the sanitary conditions of Bristol.

was obstructed with all kinds of filth. Even the graveyards, crammed into densely populated areas, were overflowing.[7]

The Rural Dean of the Diocese of Bristol provided a statement to Clark's report.[8] The Dean was as much concerned with the moral as the physical health of the overcrowded population. He observed that poor housing and overcrowding went hand in hand with 'vice and wretchedness'.

'How could the inhabitants,' he asked , '... be decent and orderly, when they are compelled to live, by day and by night, in rooms crowded with persons, many of them of the most abandoned character, from the sight of whose disgusting habits and the hearing of whose blasphemous and obscene words they have no escape?'[9] Cleanliness was literally next to godliness.

What happened next was truly impressive. Over the following 15 years an integrated city-wide sewerage system was constructed. Bristol was divided into five districts – Clifton Higher Level; Bedminster; Clifton Lower Level; St Philip's and Frome Valley – which were tackled one at a time. In the low lying area of St Paul's there were concerns that the brick built sewers would leak and contaminate local wells. The famous London sanitary engineer Joseph Bazalgette (1819-91) was brought in to advise and recommended the use of Portland cement.[10]

Some householders were reluctant, or unable, to pay for the connection of their house drains to the new sewer. 'Gentlemen, take care of your pockets,' warned *The Bristol Mirror*.[11]

By 1865, over 80 miles of mains sewers had been dug under the streets of Bristol. Sewage was discharged into the tidal Cut and the Avon at six different points. It wasn't an ideal solution. The filth had merely been moved to a less populous area. The problem of disposing of untreated sewage once it had been collected was yet to be addressed.

In addition, in 1867, the city appointed a 'sanitary detective force' of four district health inspectors.[12] They were aided by eight assistants, whose remit was to seek out and remedy unsanitary conditions by white-liming and disinfecting buildings and out-houses. The reek of filth was replaced by the smell of carbolic acid poured down drains.

With regards to rubbish collection, it was proudly reported in 1875 that the principal thoroughfares were swept and cleansed daily, the others two or three times a week. Scavengers' carts made regular rounds to pick up rubbish and house ash.[13] Large iron boxes, dustbins, for ashes were also placed near the more populous courts and alleys. There were also unofficial street sweepers. Young lads ready to make a quick penny kept the local market gardens supplied with cart loads of manure.

The consequences were dramatic. When another cholera epidemic swept the country in 1868 Bristol escaped lightly. While many cities suffered severely, in Bristol there were only 49 cases, 29 of which were fatal.[14]

These measures also made financial sense for the Corporation. A reduction in the disease led to a fall in the poor rate. Problems did remain – primarily, how to treat waste matter before it was put back into the environment. As late as 1964, chlorine gas in solution was being injected into the Avon to neutralise the offensive odour caused by the decomposition of the sewage.

Baths and Washhouses

The first public bath and wash house was opened at Broad Weir, St Jude's in 1850. There was a massive demand: 7,352 people used the facilities in the first four weeks.

By 1906 there were seven Corporation bathhouses open to the public:

- Broad Weir, opened 1850.
- Mayor's Paddock, corner of Clarence Road and Mayor Street, Redcliffe, opened 1873.
- Jacob's Wells, opened 1889.
- Rennison's Baths, Montpelier, acquired 1892. Originally opened in the 1760s as a private *Pleasure Bath*. Closed 1916.
- The Royal, Kingsdown – acquired 1897.
- Victoria Baths, Oakfield Road, Clifton, opened 1850. Acquired by the Corporation in 1897. Re-opened in 2008 as Clifton Lido restaurant.
- Barton Hill Baths, opened 1903.

The charges for the baths, which could be hot, cold, shower or swimming, ranged from one penny to sixpence.

At the Broad Weir and Mayor's Paddock there were also laundries. Hot and cold water, a drying space and an iron were provided for one penny an hour.

Jacob's Wells Baths also had a swimming pool. But this was only for men. Women weren't allowed to swim until 1895, and that was just for one afternoon a week.

'Swimming baths are now in the course of construction at three of the public parks, viz Ashton, Victoria and Eastville.' *Dictionary of Bristol,* Arrowsmith, 1906.

There was also a privately owned Turkish bath at the bottom of Park Street. 'One of the largest Turkish Baths in England'.

In 1922 a campaign won the right for mixed bathing in some of the swimming pools, but not all.

On the reverse of this 1908 postcard, J Perrett of Redland is invited by a grandchild to throw away his walking sticks and, like the angels, to experience the soothing effects of the Turkish Baths!

THE SWEETEST AND MOST WHOLESOME WATERS

- Water supply -

These days we take for granted the miracle of fresh, clean water instantly on tap. It hasn't always been so.

In early times there was never a shortage of water in Bristol. Besides the Rivers Avon and Frome, fed by numerous brooks, there were also many springs gushing from the hillsides offering fresh, clean drinking water.

During the thirteenth and fourteenth centuries, largely thanks to the monks from a number of monasteries that were dotted around the edge of Bristol at the time, water from several of these springs was brought into the city through a sophisticated system of conduits.

A conduit from a spring in Knowle took water to St Mary Redcliffe, and St John's Hospital opposite, and then down to Temple Street. To the north of the city, the Quay Pipe, the main water supply for ships, was fed by a spring two miles away on Ashley Hill. It would have been from the Quay Pipe that John and Sebastian Cabot filled their barrels of drinking water in preparation for their courageous voyages of discovery. The water from a spring on Brandon Hill was diverted through a conduit that ran down what is now Park Street to the Carmelite Friary – where the Bristol Beacon (formerly Colston Hall) now stands. In 1367, this conduit was extended downhill to St John's Church. The water from these pipes was available to anyone free of charge. Citizens could queue to fill a pot, or could pay someone to collect the water for them.

It is remarkable that, 750 years after the

Citizens could queue to fill a pot, or could pay someone to collect the water for them. Temple Conduit, 1822. © Bristol Culture (Bristol Museum & Art Gallery).

spigot was set into St John's Church wall, water still flows. Indeed, after the bombing of the centre of Bristol during the Second World War, it was one of the few water sources that continued to run.

In medieval times the waters of the Avon were clean enough for clothes to be washed in. William of Worcester wrote in 1480: 'sometimes I have seen 12 women at a time… at the river Avon washing woollen cloths and other household items.'[15]

Worcester did, however, note that the best

A conduit from a spring in Knowle took water to St Mary Redcliffe.

water came with the flow of the tide: 'For the goodwives, when the tide there flows back into the sea, so that the river Avon coming from Bristol Bridge shall be clear and fresh, so then do they do their washing at (those) particular times of the day.'

Up to the eighteenth century Bristol was said to have one of the best water supplies of any city in the kingdom. 'The sweetest and most wholesome waters from pumps and conduits placed in every street are to be had in great plenty,' wrote William Matthews in his *Directory* of 1793.[16]

But by the beginning of the nineteenth century, as the population grew, the demand for water began to exceed supply. In 1845, Sir Henry de la Beche's *Report on the state of Bristol* came to the shocking conclusion that: 'There are few if any large towns in England in which the supply of water is so inadequate as at Bristol.'[17]

The Merchant Venturers Company had already seen an opportunity. In 1844, they'd drawn up a proposal whereby the waters from the Black Rock Spring in the Avon Gorge would be tapped and its water pumped by a steam engine to a reservoir by the observatory on the Downs.[18] From there water could be piped to all the houses in Clifton. The proposal was rejected by the Council as it was far too parochial. A scheme was needed that also included the poorer, more densely populated parts of the city.

Two years later, in 1846, the Bristol Waterworks Company was formed. Local business people, including members of the Fry and George families, were among the 272 subscribers. The scheme involved bringing water from various springs in the Mendips through an impressive 16km iron pipe called the 'Line of Works' to a reservoir at Barrow Gurney. From Barrow Gurney the water flowed by gravity to two service reservoirs – one at Bedminster Down, the other just off Whiteladies Road. From Whiteladies Road water was pumped to a third reservoir on the Downs (next to the water tower – built in 1956) which, at 100m high, served the more elevated parts of the city.[19] These reservoirs, now discretely grassed over, continue to function today.

Yet they were not in time to stop a further devastating epidemic of Cholera in 1849.

In the end, getting water to every household was a slow and protracted process. The summer months of 1864 saw a drought and supplies were limited to one or two hours a day; in some parts of the city they dried up altogether.

Even so, by 1866, it was claimed that nearly every house was connected to the mains water system. In 1875, Mr D. Davies, the Medical Officer for Health for Bristol, was pleased to comment that the hardness of the water, which was moderate, was 'well adapted to tea making, a point of considerable importance to thrifty householders'.[20] More important, however, was the fact that the death rate in the city from diarrhoea was now the lowest in England.

The demand for sources of clean water was ever increasing. The River Yeo was dammed in 1890s to form the Blagdon Reservoir; the Cheddar Reservoir dates back to the 1930s, while the Chew Valley Reservoir – the fifth largest artificial lake in the United Kingdom – was created in 1956.

During the Great Drought of 1976 the Mendip reservoirs were so low that they began to resemble paddling pools. Between 27 June

After the bombing of the centre of Bristol during the Second World War this tap, by the wall of St John's Church, was one of the few water sources that continued to flow.

and 7 July the maximum daily temperature never dropped below 31 degrees centigrade. There was a hosepipe ban and consumers were encouraged to 'save water and bath with a friend'. Plans were considered seriously to harpoon an iceberg from the Arctic and tow it to Avonmouth Docks. The end of the drought was heralded by massive thunderstorms during the August Bank Holiday.

Today, Bristol Water supplies over a million customers. Approximately 50 per cent of its water continues to come from the Mendip region. The other 50 per cent is piped from the River Severn. The water is purified by 16 treatment works across the area. Treatment includes filtration to clean the water and the use of chemicals such as chlorine to disinfect.

A Sacred Jewish Spring

In 1987, what is thought to be a sacred Jewish spring, possibly a Mikveh[21], was re-discovered at the rear of a building on Jacobs Wells Road. Dating from 1100, it is claimed to be the oldest known Mikveh in Europe.

PUBLIC HEALTH

THE THIRD UNHEALTHIEST CITY IN ENGLAND

- Parks and open spaces -

Adequate open and green space can be an important health-giving and energising element of the city landscape. Unfortunately, as we have seen, the 1845 *Royal Commission on the Health of Towns* branded Bristol as the third unhealthiest city in England.[22] Bristol was overcrowded with few public spaces. The acrid air was thick not just from the soot of domestic chimneys but also from a range of noxious industrial processes. Apart from Durdham Down, there were only six public parks and squares in which people could seek sanctuary from the rough pavements and incessant grime of the city.

Over the next 50 years matters were to change. The Public Health Act of 1848 empowered local Boards of Health to provide, maintain and improve land for parks.[24] In 1861, free access was allowed to the Downs after the Merchant Venturers surrendered their rights to the land. A number of other plots of land were donated to the council specifically to be laid out as public parks.

Bristol's public parks and open spaces in 1847[23]

With Brandon Hill given to the corporation in 1174 Bristol claims to have one of the oldest municipal open spaces in the country.
- Brandon Hill (19.5 acres).
- Queen Square (6.75 acres).
- College Green (4.5 acres).
- Portland Square (2.25 acres).
- Brunswick Square (1.25 acres).
- King Square (1.0 acre).

Nine feet long and weighing nearly three tons, this captured Russian cannon took up its new position on Brandon Hill on 19 August, 1857. It was more than capable of accommodating these Bristol children.

Bristol's Victorian and Edwardian parks were characterised by winding asphalt paths, rockeries, circular bandstands, drinking fountains, toilets and tempting swathes of lawn.

Bristol's Victorian and Edwardian parks were characterised by winding asphalt paths, rockeries, circular bandstands, drinking fountains, toilets and tempting swathes of lawn adorned with signs 'Keep off the grass'.

Massive cannons were a popular climbing feature. There were two cannons on Brandon Hill, trophies from the Crimean Campaign (1853-56), while those in Victoria and Eastville parks came from the training ship *HMS Deadalus*[25]. Along with much of the city's railings, they were subsequently melted down during the Second World War.

During the twentieth century the council bought the estates of Blaise Castle (650 acres) in 1926; Oldbury Court (115 acres) in 1936; Arnos Court (19 acres) in 1948; Ashton Court (850 acres) in 1959 and Kings Weston (300 acres) in 1996.

In the 1960s, rather than redevelop the blitzed area of Castle Street, the ground was landscaped and redesigned as an 'oasis in the heart of the city'. Within Castle Park are the scattered remains of Bristol Castle including walls and vaults, as well as the fire-gutted St Peter's Church. In 1993, the council commissioned sculptures by Peter Randall Page and Kate Malone to augment the water feature to the east of the church.

Parks continue to be established and upgraded. In 2002, Hengrove Park was opened and hailed as the biggest play park in the South of England. The days of the resident park warden, however, are long gone. During present cash-strapped times parks and many green spaces are now looked after by voluntary organisations.

- Some parks and open spaces -

Ashton Court Estate. 850 acres. The house and estate was originally owned by the Smyth family. The last Smyth to live there died in 1946. After 13 years of neglect the estate was acquired by the council in 1959.

Badocks Wood, Southmead. 30 acres. Donated by Sir Stanley Badock in 1937. Ancient woodland, wildflower meadows and a bronze-age tumulus.

Brandon Hill, Clifton. 19.5 acres. Contains defensive ditches thrown up during the Civil War (1642-51) and Cabot Tower (1898). The top of the hill is adorned by ornamental gardens with a rockery and pools which in the spring are home to newts and frog-spawn.

Brunswick Cemetery Gardens, St Paul's. Two acres. The cemetery was established around 1770 and later became a Unitarian burial ground until 1963. The cemetery retains a number of historic features including monuments, boundary walls and a Georgian mortuary chapel. Since the mid-1980s the cemetery has been used as a public park. It was extensively re-landscaped in 2010.

College Green, bottom of Park Street. Originally a hillock owned by St Augustine's Abbey. It was levelled and planted in 1703. It is still owned by Bristol Cathedral.

Colston Avenue (The Centre). This area of urban open space was formed when the Frome was covered over in 1893. Remodelling in 1999 caused much controversy. Once the initial shock of change wore off it was widely admired.

Cotham Gardens, Cotham. 2.5 acres. A gift from the Fry family, opened in 1880. Its extension, Cotham Avenue (Lovers Walk), was not needed by the newly established school in Redland Court and was added in 1882.

Dame Emily Park, Bedminster. Five acres. Donated by Dame Emily Smyth for a children's playground on the site of the former Dean Lane Colliery, which closed in 1906.

Eastville Park. 70 acres. Established 1889. It also had a swimming pool, opened in 1905. This is now a neglected sunken garden. The lake was dug as part of a job creation scheme during the winter of 1908-09.

Greville Smyth Park. 21.5 acres. Established 1882. Originally called 'The People's Park of Bedminster'. Bowling Green opened 1908.

Fine London Plane trees in Mina Road Park, opened 1886.

Ornate Gallic-style pissoir in Mina Road Park. There's another on Horfield Common. The Victorians installed a number of urinals across Bristol. The women just had to hold it in!

Mina Road Park. Three acres. Initially known as Hunt's Recreation Ground, named after William Hunt, donor of the land – adjoining Mina Road and Cowmead Wall – 1886. Extended in 1890. The culverted Cutlers Mills Brook merges with Horfield Brook, though the join is difficult to spot. In the south east corner of the park is an ornate, though sadly neglected, cast-iron Victorian urinal, similar to that on Horfield Common.

Montpelier Park. One acre. This pocket park was established on the site of the former St Andrew's Church which was demolished in the 1960s.

Proctor's Walk. Not a park as such, but a 'boulevard' along the south side of The Cut. The money was provided by Alderman Thomas Proctor in 1873, who paid for the planting of trees and placed benches at regular intervals. Unfortunately, the idea of perambulations alongside The Cut never took off.

Redcliffe Hill. 0.5 acre. One of Bristol's smaller parks. Now a dark and rather insalubrious corner. Tucked away off Redcliffe Hill many walk past this little oasis without noticing. For 300 years Quakers used the land for their burial ground. There is a small cave in the cliff that is said to have been home in the Middle Ages for a hermit called Thomas Sparke. The land was given to the council in the 1960s when the Redcliffe roundabout was built. It was planted with scented shrubs as a garden for the blind.

St Matthias' Park. 1.5 acres. In the eighteenth century this plot of land was named Captain Parson's Field. Later, it was used as a burial ground alongside slum dwellings for itinerant workers. In the 1880s the slums were cleared and the park opened.

Spark Evans Park, St Philips. 7.25 acres. A forlorn park popular with dog walkers from the Bristol Dogs Home. Established 1902.

St Andrew's Park. Built in 1895 as part of the St Andrews Park Estate.

St Andrew's Park. 11 acres. Built in 1895 as part of the St Andrews Park Estate. This popular park was laid out with walks and a bandstand (demolished). It is the only Bristol park to have a functioning, and well used, paddling pool. Hooray for Fay's lovely café!

St George's Park. 38 acres. Opened in 1897. Built on the fields round Fire Engine Farm. The Wain Brook was dammed to create the boating lake. A bandstand (demolished) looked on. Contains a fine avenue of London plain trees.

Victoria Park. 51.5 acres. Five separate plots of land were purchased to make this large park. Opened in 1891. An outdoor swimming pool was built in 1905. Filled in during the 1970s and used as a bowling green.

Victory Park. Presented to the Parish of Brislington by Mr and Mrs Joseph Cooke Hurle of Brislington Hill House in commemoration of peace after the First World War.

PUBLIC HEALTH

Old Sneed Park. An inky black ornamental pond, mighty oaks and grassy meadows that lead down towards the Avon.

The lost gardens of Bishop's Knoll. A series of secret overgrown terraces, belvederes, and steep steps dating back to the nineteenth century.

- Edgelands -

A recent trend is for those forgotten corners of the city – unnoticed except by dog-walkers, blackberry pickers and motor bike joy riders – to be designated as community spaces or nature reserves. Inner city wild spaces are at a premium, especially, when there is a whisper of property developers taking an interest. In such cases the previously neglected 'edgeland' swiftly becomes a community resource.

Some 'Green Spaces', Community Gardens and Nature Reserves.

Callington Road Nature Reserve, Knowle (2003). Surplus allotment land from a hospital development. Includes a dewpond, natural habitat, native trees and shrub planting.

Easter Garden, Wesley Place, off the top of Blackboy Hill (1997). A handkerchief of land planted with shrubs and fruit trees.

Hartcliffe Millenium Green, (1999). Community garden, orchard, performance area. Play area added 2010.

Narroways, St Werburgh's, (2000). Designated a Millennium Green in 2000, and an official Local Nature Reserve in 2016. Dramatic sculpted slopes from railway cuttings support herb-rich unimproved grassland with spectacular views over the city.

Old Sneed Park, (2020). An inky black ornamental pond, mighty oaks and grassy meadows lead down towards the Avon. Equally as interesting are the adjoining lost gardens of Bishops Knoll.

Bishop's Knoll, a series of secret overgrown terraces, steep steps and belvederes dating back to the nineteenth century. Managed by Woodland Trust volunteers.

The Northern Slopes are between Knowle, Knowle West and Bedminster in south Bristol and all offer spectacular views across the city. A nature reserve of three areas of green space with meadows, hedgerows and woods.

THE DOWNS

- 'The people's park' -

'Here the labouring mechanic accompanied with his faithful wife and little prattlers take their Sunday walk or summer evening excursion...' *Felix Farley's Journal*, 1760.

Bristol's famous Downs, geologically a limestone pavement, have long been a place of popular recreation. Common land for many centuries, the Downs were used for grazing sheep and cattle. Today, wild goats browse Walcombe Slade, a rocky gulley leading down to the gorge. While largely flat and windswept, the 'dumps' by Upper Belgrave Road are said to be evidence of shallow lead workings from Roman times.[26]

The Downs are made up of two areas: Durdham Down (212 acres) to the North East and Clifton Down (230 acres) to the South. On the plateau the dividing line is marked by occasional boundary stones. Prior to its establishment as a people's park, Durdham Down was owned by the Lords of the Manor of Henbury and the Society of Merchant

Between 1718 and 1813 there were regular May Day horse races on the Downs. It was a popular event with a fairground atmosphere. Later in the day, bare knuckle pugilists would attract enthusiastic crowds.
Rolinda Sharples © Bristol Culture (Bristol Museum & Art Gallery)

Venturers.[27]

During the Hotwell's heyday it was a popular place for a constitutional walk or a therapeutic drive in a horse-drawn carriage. A favourite destination for courting couples, the more remote corners of the Downs allowed for all sorts of indiscrete pleasures.

The Downs have always been a natural place for public entertainment. Between 1718 and 1813 there were regular May Day horse races. 'Though the quality of the animals was indifferent, the affair attracted a great attendance'.[28] It was a popular event with a fairground atmosphere. A temporary central grandstand built of wood and canvas was surrounded by numerous tents and booths. The side shows pulled in the crowds as much as the horseracing. Later in the day, bare knuckle pugilists would attract enthusiastic crowds.[29]

Those who could, watched the races from the safety and comfort of their carriage. Rolinda Sharples's (1793-1838) lively painting *Clifton Race-Course* [30] shows a group of wealthy ladies in bonnets, in an open-topped landau, surrounded by a sea of picnickers, pedlars and gamblers. Nearby, a boy, cap in hand, parades a dog with a saddle and a monkey dressed as a jockey. Meanwhile, a gentleman appears to be having his pocket picked.

The 1861 Act of Parliament ensured free public access. Subsequently, the Downs were, and still are, managed by the Downs Committee with representatives from both the City and the Society of Merchant Venturers.

In 1897, there was a proposal to build a tower overlooking Avon Gorge to celebrate the 400th anniversary of John Cabot's voyage to North America.[31] Discussions about on-going maintenance and other bureaucratic concerns brought the project to a halt. The commemorative tower was eventually built on Brandon Hill; in retrospect, probably a more suitable location.

The eponymous White Tree was painted, many generations ago, as a way marker. The tree, originally whitewashed to guide travellers on dark nights across the empty Downs has been replanted and repainted several times. It has saved many an innocent traveller from straying onto nearby Ladies Mile, a notorious haunt of sex workers, voyeurs and ne'er-do-wells.

Rare Plants

The Downs and Avon Gorge are host to several plants found nowhere else in the world. There are also other rare or nationally scarce species, including

- Autumn Squill (Scilla autumnalis).
- Bristol Rock-Cress (Arabis scabra).
- Fingered Sedge (Carex digitata).
- Pale St. John's-Wort (Hypericum montanum).
- Rock Stonecrop (Sedum fosterianum).
- Round-Headed Leek (Allium sphaerocephalon).
- Western Spiked Speedwell (Veronica spicata subsp. hybrid).

The Avon Gorge is significant for the emergence, since the end of the last ice age, of new species of Whitebeams, eg. Bristol Whitebeam (Sorbus bristoliensis) and Houston's Whitebeam (Sorbus x houstoniae) named in 2005, after the poet, botanist and rock climber, Libby Houston.[32]

SCARLET LYCHNIS
- Bristol's Flower -

Until recently a flowerbed was set aside in the Mall Gardens, Clifton, for the Scarlet Lychnis, Bristol's flower.

This unassuming plant is also called 'The Flower of Candia', the 'Campion of Constantinople' but most commonly 'Nonesuch'.

The Scarlet Lychnis (*Lychnis Chalcedonica*) is not a native British plant. Exactly why and when it was chosen as Bristol's floral emblem is uncertain. It is said to have been brought to Bristol in the Middle Ages by returning crusaders from the Middle East.

The flower can also be seen in the University of Bristol's Botanic Gardens, Stoke Bishop, along with a range of flora unique to Bristol.

ENDNOTES

1. Large, D. and Round, F. *Public Health in Mid-Victorian Bristol*, 1974, Bristol Branch of the Historical Association, p.3.
2. Ibid., p.1.
3. Whitfield, M., *The Bristol Microscopists and the Cholera Epidemic of 1849*, 2011, Avon Local History and Archaeology, p.5.
4. Clark, G. T., *Report to the General Board of Health*, 1850, For Her Majesty's Stationery Office.
5. ibid. p.17.
6. Arrowsmith, J.W., *Arrowsmith's Dictionary of Bristol*, 1906, Bristol, p.328.
7. Clark, G.T., op. cit., p.18.
8. ibid., p. 47-49.
9. ibid., p.48.
10. Large, D. and Round, F. op. cit., p.7.
11. ibid., p.5.
12. ibid. p.17.
13. British Association. *Bristol and its Environs*. 1875, J Wright and Co, p.207.
14. Large, D. and Round, F. op. cit., p.18.
15. Bettey, J., *William Worcestre – The Topography of Medieval Bristol*, 2000, Bristol Record Society, Vol 51, p.43.
16. Matthews, W. *Bristol Directory*, 1793, Bristol, (facsimile edition) p.45.
17. Large, D. and Round, F., op. cit. p.3.
18. Latimer, J. *Annals of Bristol - Nineteenth Century*, 1887, Bristol, p.144.
19. Clarke.G.T., op.cit., p.115.
20. Anon., *Bristol and Its Environs*, 1875, London, p.305.
21. A mikveh is a bath for ritual immersion in Judaism.
22. Large, D. and Round, F., op.cit., p.1.
23. Lambert, D.. *Historic Public Parks - Bristol*. 2000, Avon Gardens Trust, p.3.
24. Young, C. *The Making of Bristol's Victorian Parks* in *Transactions of the Bristol and Gloucestershire Archaelogical Society*, Volume 116 (1998), p.175-84.
25. *Western Daily Press*, 10 October 1904.
26. Branigan.K., *The Romans in the Bristol Area*, 1969, Bristol Branch of the Historical Association, p.14.
27. Young, C., *op. cit.*, p.174.
28. Latimer, J. *Annals of Bristol - Nineteenth Century*, 1887, Bristol, p.127.
29. ibid.,p.97.
30. On display in M Shed Museum.
31. Nichols, G. *Clifton and Durdham Downs: A Place of Public Resort and Recreation*, 2006, Bristol Branch of the Historical Association, p. 21.
32. Barton, M., *Dizzy Heights*, in *Bristol Review of Books*, 2010, Issue 13, p.18-9.

HOSPITALS

FROM THE CRADLE TO THE GRAVE

- Bristol's hospitals -

After the Second World War, the new Welfare State offered free medical support to all from the cradle to the grave. Before the introduction of the National Health Service in 1948 hospitals were privately run. Apart from a few services specifically supported by charitable donation, any treatment had to be paid for.

Those who could afford it would take out private health insurance, while some institutions would offer their own subscription service.

The provision offered by the Bristol Dispensary, Castle Green, in 1906 was typical:

'A subscriber of one guinea (£1.05 p) receives a book of notes containing five sick notes... one midwifery note (which may be used as a sick note) and two notes of recommendation entitling the bearer of each note to medical attendance on payment of five shillings on presenting it at the dispensary or any branch of it. A donation of £21 constitutes a life subscription...'[1]

The Bristol Medical Mission, 7 Redcross Street, off Old Market, was run as a charity and offered a more 'open door' policy.

Bristol Royal Infirmary, Marlborough Street. Established 1735. The 'Royal' prefix was bestowed by Queen Victoria in 1850.

'The sick are admitted without notes and are allowed to see the doctor in the order in which they arrive in the morning. Patients are expected to bring bottles for the medicine they require...Patients who are quite unable to come to the dispensary are visited at their homes by the doctor on Tuesdays, Thursdays and Saturdays.'[2]

In 1875, the Bristol Corporation maintained an ambulance that could be used by qualified medical practitioners free of charge. (The doctor had to provide a horse and driver!) The interior of the carriage was lined with American leather which could be scrubbed and disinfected with Sulphuric Acid Gas every time it was used.[3]

At the beginning of the twentieth century the principal medical charities were:[4]

- Bristol Royal Infirmary, Marlborough Street. Established 1735. The 'Royal' suffix was bestowed by Queen Victoria in 1850.
- Bristol General Hospital, Guinea Street, Redcliffe. Established 1832.
- Bristol Dispensary, Castle Green. Established 1775. The Dispensary also had a branch at Malago Road, Bedminster.
- The Bristol Eye Hospital, Lower Maudlin Street. Established 1810. It was the third hospital in the country to devote itself entirely to the treatment of the eye.

By now, the lesson about quarantine had been well learnt. There was a hospital ship at Avonmouth for the quarantine of infected people disembarking at the Port of Bristol. There were also isolation hospitals at Clift House, Bedminster and Novers Hill, while Ham Green Fever Hospital, opened 1899, was set aside for those suffering from smallpox and other contagious diseases. Prior to this there was a small fever and smallpox isolation establishment inappropriately situated at the west end of Feeder Road.[5]

Cossham Memorial Hospital, Lodge Hill, Kingswood, endowed by the wealthy mine owner Handel Cossham, was opened in 1907.

In the 1930s W.D. and H.O. Wills ran their own Respiratory Hospital on top of the Mendip Hills for those who were affected by the dusty working conditions and, more likely, the free cigarette allowance for employees.

Bristol Homeopathic Hospital
The Hahnemann Hospital, Brunswick Square, offered homeopathic treatments from about 1880. The Hospital, renamed the Bristol Homeopathic Hospital, relocated to new buildings at the top of St Michaels Hill in 1925. The buildings were designed by George Oatley and funded by Walter Melville Wills in memory of his son, Robert, who was killed in the First World War.[6]

The hospital joined the National Health Service in 1948. Therapies ceased to be offered from the building in 2015 amid increasing controversy around the effectiveness of homeopathic treatment.

'MATRON FINDS IT NECESSARY FOR HER HEALTH TO USE A LITTLE PORTER'

- Bristol General Hospital -

Even before the cholera outbreak in 1831 it had become clear that the medical facilities provided by the Bristol Infirmary (established 1735) were overstretched. A new hospital was required to support the growing population of south Bristol and Bedminster.

With this in mind a group – many of whom were Quakers – came together to promote the establishment of the Bristol General Hospital. Understandably, there was opposition from the Board of the Infirmary who feared they would lose subscribers. Nevertheless, after a survey of sites in the city, suitable premises were found in Guinea Street. The property consisted of a house that had previously been an 'academy' and other buildings and sheds that had been used as warehouses.

The site was well placed to serve the growing population of south Bristol. The situation, near The Cut and 100 metres from the Bathurst Basin, was described as 'airy'. 'There is no building to interrupt the fresh air which accompanies every influx of the tide'.[7] There was one objection, however – its closeness to Acraman's Anchor Works. Concern was expressed that the constant hammering and clattering from the forge, as well as the fumes, would have a far from recuperative effect on the patients. A sub-committee was appointed to look into this, but it reported that any such fears were unfounded. Furthermore they declared the site to be 'particularly salubrious and desirable'.

The property was adapted to hospital use and a well was sunk that could provide 200

The new General Hospital was opened in 1858. There was a bathroom with hot and cold water on each floor, a steam driven lift, speaking tubes and even heating in the passageways.

Another novel feature of the General Hospital was that the ground floor was designed and let as a warehouse.

gallons of water an hour. Lighting by coal-gas was installed.

There was a slight delay in the appointment of staff due to 'the disturbed state of public affairs'. With the cholera outbreak, the riots in Queen Square and a general state of national

The General Hospital in around 1900.

unrest because of the reform bill, 1831 was hardly an auspicious year for new ventures.

A matron, three doctors, four surgeons and an apothecary were eventually engaged. The matron was supported by a number of untrained nurses. The hospital was formally opened on 1 November, 1832. From the beginning the 20 beds were well used. Indeed, with up to 40 in-patients being looked after at any one time, beds frequently had to be shared. Even though there was still no understanding of bacteria or anaesthetics the patients were at least well fed. The meals provided were substantial:

- *Breakfast: 6ozs. of bread. 1 pint of tea.*
- *Dinner: 6ozs. of meat and potatoes, four days a week. 1 quart of broth, and 12 ozs. of boiled rice on other days. 1 pint of beer.*
- *Supper: 6ozs. of bread. 1 pint of gruel.*[8]

Doctors were trained to as high a standard as medical knowledge would allow, but in the days before Florence Nightingale the quality of nursing was not high. The matron's job was said to be particularly demanding – so much so that she requested a supply of beer to steady her nerves: 'The matron finds it necessary for her health to use a little porter', the hospital committee was told. Accordingly, three dozen pint bottles of beer were ordered for the matron's use.

Patients were warned by notices that they must be clean and 'if insubordinate' were liable to be dismissed and refused re-admission. Visiting days could be noisy: a notice was put up encouraging visitors to be quiet.

Within ten years of opening, facilities at the hospital became overstretched: a reflection of the fast-growing urban population, and the increasing number of causalities from the nearby factories, docks and collieries.

In 1840, the number of in-patients was 396, while out-patients numbered 2,926. By the

1850s finances were on a sure enough footing for new purpose-built premises to be planned. At last, in 1851, the incessant noise from the anchor works was silenced when Acraman's land was bought for the further development of the hospital.

Patients were transferred to the new building on 3 August 1858. Compared with the rudimentary Guinea Street premises the new hospital was a showpiece. Designed by Bristol architect William Bruce Gingell, two four-storey blocks were built: one facing the New Cut, the other the Bathurst Basin. There was a bathroom with hot and cold water on each floor, a steam driven lift, speaking tubes and even heating in the passageways. The wards had open fires and wooden floors; the walls were whitewashed and hung with pictures. Another novel feature of the hospital was that the ground floor was designed and let as a warehouse. It was hoped that the prime storage space so close to Bathurst Basin would generate extra income for the hospital.

In 1873, a new out-patients department was added, while Oatley and Thomas built, in 1914, a south-facing wing with open air balconies. Once again, the quality of the situation was commented upon. 'It affords uninterrupted sunshine and air, and has an excellent outlook,' reported *The Building News*.[9]

In 2012, after over 180 years of service, the Bristol General Hospital closed its doors. The facilities provided by the 'General' were transferred to the South Bristol Community Hospital at Hengrove Park. The old hospital buildings have now been thoughtfully redeveloped by City and Country, with some of the later, less sympathetic, additions to the building removed. As ever, the excellence of the situation has been a selling point, 'Many of the apartments benefit from water facing or courtyard views', says the sales website for what is now called *The General*. The warehouse space under the building is set aside for restaurants and businesses.

Bristol's Nobel Prize Winner Dorothy Hodgkin

Chancellor of the University of Bristol 1971 - 88.

Dorothy Hodgkin (1910-94) was a chemist who discovered the atomic structures of insulin and Vitamin B12. During the Second World War she unravelled the mysteries of penicillin for which she was awarded the Nobel Prize in 1974.[10]

'THERE IS SOMETHING TO BE LEARNED ABOUT MENTAL DISEASE EACH DAY'

- Psychiatric care -

Before the Madhouse Act of 1774, treatment of the 'insane' was an ad hoc affair. Non-licensed practitioners could run 'madhouses' as a commercial enterprise, often with little regard for the inmates. The Madhouse Act required institutions that looked after the 'insane' to be licensed and regularly inspected.[11]

For 'pauper lunatics' the prospects were not good: St Peter's Workhouse or, even worse, Newgate Prison, beckoned.

In 1808, the County Asylum Act encouraged local authorities to establish asylums for the mentally ill with funding to be collected through the rates. The Bristol Poor Law Commissioners only half-heartedly embraced the 1808 Act. They merely continued with their current informal provision at St Peter's, but made it official by setting aside a specific part of the building for 'pauper lunatics'.

The conditions were scandalously inadequate. Indeed, in 1844 the Lunacy Commissioners pronounced St Peter's as being 'totally unfit for patients'.

Eventually, a purpose-built psychiatric hospital was opened in 1861. The Bristol Lunatic Asylum, in Stapleton, next door to the Bristol Union Workhouse (formerly the French Prison, later Stapleton Hospital, now Blackberry Hill Hospital), was set in 24 acres. It was managed as a community and run on the lines of a country estate.

During the nineteenth century there had been a gradual change in the understanding of health, and the treatment of psychiatric illness. While those with mental health issues or learning difficulties were still frequently stigmatised and ridiculed, at least the Lunacy Act of 1845 specified that those needing psychiatric care should be treated as patients rather than prisoners. Indeed, with care and attention it was acknowledged that a patient's health could get better. The term 'asylum' indicated a place of protection. Asylums were to provide sanctuary, moral therapy and a regular routine.

'There are many degrees of comfort and happiness to be obtained by proper treatment; it must be done in the right way, and it must be done continuously', stated *The Handbook for the Instruction of Attendants on the Insane (1885)*, the standard reference book for those working in mental health. 'There is something to be learned about mental disease each day', wrote the authors of the handbook.

Today, under the auspices of the University of the West of England, the buildings of the former Bristol Lunatic Asylum, built in a low-key Italianate style, look comfortably grand. Inside, the white painted rooms are light and airy. This hasn't always been so. In previous times, with bars on windows, padded cells and maximum restraint facilities, the atmosphere wouldn't have been quite so appealing

Even so, the benefits of these new surroundings were obvious. Commissioners visiting in 1861 said 'they could hardly recognise the patients before them as the same company they had been accustomed to seeing at St Peter's Hospital'.[12]

That may have been the case. But it was cheaper to keep patients in the workhouse than the new asylum. Research shows that 'lunatics' continued to be sent to the Eastville Workhouse where there were wards specifically designated for the 'insane', 'imbeciles' and 'epileptics'.[13] Even in 1881, 20 years after the Bristol Lunatic Asylum had been opened, 15 per cent of Eastville Workhouse's 1,068 residents were classified as 'lunatics'.[14]

Suitable work was an important part of the treatment in the asylum. Wherever possible patients were employed on the farm or in the landscaped gardens or occupied in regular domestic work in the houses. The asylum had its own bakery, piggery, blacksmiths and shoe making shop. Fresh vegetables were available from the kitchen gardens. 'Employment is both profitable and curative' wrote Dr Stephenson, the Asylum's first medical director. 'From 1861 to 1900, 48 per cent of the people admitted left recovered or relieved. More left within a year of admission'.[15]

During the First World War the Bristol Lunatic Asylum was requisitioned as a military hospital, changing its name to the Beaufort War Hospital. Three months were spent converting the buildings to accommodate up to 1,500 wounded soldiers. The previous residents were transferred to asylums across the South West, though 40 patients stayed behind as workers. Some unfortunates were even sent back to St Peter's Workhouse.

One of the medical orderlies working at the Beaufort War Hospital was the artist Stanley Spencer (1891-1959). 'For ten months he did little more than scrub floors, bandage convalescent soldiers and cart supplies around the vast lunatic asylum-cum-hospital'.[16] The murals at Sandham Memorial Chapel, Burghclere, said to be one of the great achievements of twentieth century painting,

The Bristol Lunatic Asylum, built in a low-key Italianate style, looked comfortably grand.

are claimed to have been partially inspired by Spencer's stay at the Beaufort.[17]

In 1930, the Bristol Lunatic Asylum changed its name to Bristol Mental Hospital. By now the Victorian facilities were clearly inadequate. With over 1,250 patients, the institution had become gravely overcrowded.

A new purpose-built Mental Hospital was officially opened at Barrow Gurney in 1939.[18] The design, by George Oatley, was considered progressive. 'The hospital is built on the villa system which breaks away from the institution atmosphere'.[19]

With the Mental Health Act of 1959, it was decided that, with the availability of more effective medicines, large institutions were no longer the best way to care for patients. The introduction of the Community Care Programme, whereby large institutions were closed, was first announced by Enoch Powell, the Health Secretary, in 1961. Powell described asylums as 'doomed institutions'.[20] But with limited resources it would be over 40 years before the 'Community Care' vision was fully implemented in Bristol.

Meanwhile, 'mental' as a term for a psychiatric hospital was dropped. In 1960, staff and patients chose the name Glenside, reflecting its position above a glen through which the neighbouring Frome flowed.

Glenside eventually closed in 1994 and is now part of the University of the West of England's Glenside Campus, housing the Faculty for Health and Social Care. The fascinating Glenside Hospital Museum (www.glensidemuseum.org.uk) is housed in the old chapel.

Similarly, Barrow Gurney Hospital closed in 2008. The buildings, derelict for almost a decade, were eventually demolished in 2018. The site is now home to a residential development.

Stoke Park
For those with learning difficulties there was the Stoke Park Colony (1909-2000) across the Frome valley. A number of buildings were lined up on the ridge behind Stoke Park House. It was the largest group of hospitals for those with learning difficulties in the United Kingdom.

Brislington House Asylum
On the Bath Road, just outside Bristol, was one of the first privately owned asylums in the country. The fireproof (iron was substituted for wood in the construction) Palladian mansion was opened in 1806 by the Quaker Dr Edward Long Fox (1761 - 1835), who was also a physician at the Bristol Infirmary. Dr Fox pioneered the *'humane treatment of the insane'*, basically a belief in the restorative power of both nature and home comforts. Although separate blocks reflected the social standing of the occupants,[21] patients were at least made to feel at home, rather than locked up in an institution or a prison. Dr Long Fox became so celebrated for his treatment of mental illness that he was invited to Windsor Castle to advise on King George III's long-term insanity.[22]

Northwoods House, Old Gloucester Road, Winterbourne
Set up in 1836 by Dr H.H. Fox to continue the good work of his father, Edward Long Fox. Northwoods House was expressly for 'the various forms of mental infirmity occurring to the ladies and gentlemen of the upper and middle classes.' The house, which could accommodate 20 ladies and 25 gentlemen, stood in extensive grounds with more than a mile of pleasure walks. Continued as a privately run mental asylum until 1948.

Northwoods, now North Woods, has been extensively reconfigured into private residences.

BRITAIN'S FIRST WOMAN DOCTOR
- Elizabeth Blackwell -

Britain's first woman doctor, Elizabeth Blackwell[23] (1821-1910) was born at the Counterslip, Temple Back. At the age of 10 she moved with her family to North America; first to New York then to Cincinnati.

Her father, in a quixotic attempt to undermine the plantation system of the Deep South, hoped to establish sugar beet as a major crop. His plans came to little.

It was in her mid-20s that Blackwell thought of becoming a doctor. A family friend, dying of cancer, had said to her: 'if only I had been treated by a lady doctor I would not have suffered so terribly'. From that moment Elizabeth Blackwell had a mission in her life.

Convincing the medical establishment that there were places for women as doctors, not just nurses, was to be a lifelong battle. It took applications to 23 medical schools before she received an acceptance by Geneva College in New York State.

Blackwell undertook her initial training in North America, followed by further study in Paris and London. Although she excelled as a student there were still lecturers who refused to teach her. In London the Professor for Midwifery rejected her from his classes, while in Paris, she had to disguise herself to undertake dissection in the morgue.

Blackwell graduated in 1840 and became the first woman doctor in America. Her problems were to start all over again when she began to practice. Doctors – all men, of course – refused to work with her, pharmacists would not make up her prescriptions, patients were wary.

It was only slowly that she was able to build up her practice in New York, and this was largely thanks to the support of a group of Quaker women.

In the following ten years she went on to establish an infirmary for women and children, and then a college to train more women doctors.

It was in her capacity as a lecturer that Blackwell eventually returned to her city of birth. In 1869 she was invited to attend the Social Science Congress that was held in Bristol. Around the same time she decided to move back to England. In 1871 she accepted the Chair of Gynaecology at the newly founded London School of Medicine.

Along with her friend Florence Nightingale she was an avid promoter of cleanliness and hygiene. Even more controversial were her writings on sex education.

Blackwell died in Hastings, Sussex, in 1910 at the age of 89. 1n 2013, The University of Bristol's Health Research Institute was named in honour of Blackwell.

ENDNOTES

1. Arrowsmith, J.W., *Arrowsmith's Dictionary of Bristol*, 1906, Bristol, pp.217- 8.
2. Arrowsmith, J.W., op. cit., p.219.
3. British Association. *Bristol and its Environs*, 1875, J Wright and Co, p.313.
4. Arrowsmith, J.W., op. cit., p.217-25.
5. See Bristol Ordinance Survey map, 1844-1888. http://maps.bristol.gov.uk/kyp/?edition=
6. Whittingham, S. *Sir George Oatley*, Redcliffe Press, 2011, p.187-91.
7. Odery Symes, J., *A Short History of the Bristol General Hospital*, 1932, Bristol. p.4.
8. ibid., p.20.
9. Whittingham, S., op. cit., p.184.
10. Gage, S. in Duffus, J., *The Women Who Built Bristol*, 2018, Tangent, p. 201-2.
11. https://www.countyasylums.co.uk/history/
12. Quote from display at Glenside Museum.
13. Ball, R., Parkin, D. and Mills, S., *100 Fishponds Road. Life and Death in a Victorian Workhouse*. 2016. Bristol Radical History Group, p.104.
14. ibid., p.106.
15. Quote from display at Glenside Museum.
16. Gough, P., *That Vile Place*. Bristol Review of Books. Issue 1, Summer 2006. pp.15-6.
17. Information from Blue Plaque at Glenside.
18. https://www.countyasylums.co.uk/barrow-hospital-barrow-gurney/
19. Whittingham, S., op. cit., p.181.
20. Penrose, S. *Images of Change*, 2007, English Heritage, p. 77.
21. https://historicengland.org.uk/listing/the-list/list-entry/1203910. Retrieved 19 November 2019.
22. Manson, M., *Riot! The Bristol Bridge Massacre of 1793*, 1997, Past & Present Press, p.100.
23. This article was originally published in the Bristol Evening Post under the pseudonym of John Houseman in the 1980s. Unfortunately my original text doesn't have a date on it! For further reading I recommend Jane Duffus's *The Women Who Built Bristol* 1184 – 2018, 2018, Tangent Books.

WHAT TO DO WITH THE DEAD?

STREWN WITH BONES

- Graveyards and Cemeteries -

What to do with the dead? There are a number of considerations: appropriate disposal of the body, suitable remembrance of the life lived and, according to belief, transition of the spirit. Or not.

Before Christianity arrived in this country burials were undertaken in a variety of ways according to the importance of the deceased. A high status individual might be buried in a long barrow such as the one in Stoke Bishop, or in a tumulus, or cremated with the ashes put into a funeral urn. The Romans buried their dead in out-of-town cemeteries, while the Anglo-Saxons practiced cremation.

Christians established graveyards around churches. Those with money would pay to be buried inside the church, sometimes in a family vault under or alongside the building. Before the Reformation, money was sometimes bequeathed to pay for a chantry, where a priest would pray specifically for the soul of the departed.

With a small population the parish graveyard was an adequate solution. But in times of plague and high mortality, mass unmarked graves were dug out of town. When the foundations for the Bristol department store Lewis's (now Primark) were excavated in 1954 graves were uncovered. There were excited rumours that these were plague burials. The more humdrum explanation is that these were ordinary graves from St James's churchyard which once extended down to the Haymarket.[1]

The location of Bristol's plague pits is a mystery. Some say they were at Dundry, but that seems too remote. The historian Anton Bantock would tell his pupils at Bedminster Down School that they were the three circular enclosures on Bedminster Down Common. But why circular? We await confirmation.

By the 1830s the population of Bristol, at 91,000 and growing, was 12 times greater than it had been in medieval times and the 61 places of burial were spilling over. There was an increasing need for hygienic graveyards set away from the centre of population. Clark, in

Arnos Vale Cemetery, modelled on the Arcadian landscaped cemeteries popular in Europe.

Arnos Vale Cemetery. Forty-five acres of open fields on the Totterdown slopes were planted with trees and shrubs.

his 1850 *Report to the General Board of Health*, wrote 'the church yards are numerous, very full, some of them in very bad order and almost all in crowded and poor neighbourhoods'.[2] Christchurch burial ground was strewn with bones, and corpses were said to be buried only three feet underground. Many of the graveyards were raised above the surrounding area and in wet weather offensive foul water was exuded from them. Consequently, in 1853, most of the church burial grounds of Bristol were ordered to be closed.

- *Some graveyards* -

Arnos Vale, Bath Road. Arnos Vale Cemetery, modelled on the Arcadian landscaped cemeteries popular in Europe, was established in 1836 by a private company, the Bristol General Cemetery Company. Forty-five acres of open fields on the Totterdown slopes were planted with trees and shrubs, laid with paths and turned into a spacious garden cemetery. Entry was through two impressive neo-classical gatehouses by Charles Underwood (1791-1883). The cemetery was opened in 1839 with chapels for both Anglicans and Non-conformists. This 'enchantingly beautiful spot'[3] was a timely and visionary initiative and although business was slow at first, with the closure of the inner-city church graveyards demand soon escalated.

A crematorium at Arnos Vale was constructed in 1928. At that time, Plymouth Crematorium excepted, it was the only crematorium in the South West of England.

In April 2001 Bristol City Council made a compulsory purchase of the cemetery which had become run-down and overgrown. It subsequently came under Council control in 2003, and is now managed by the Arnos Vale Cemetery Trust. Today, as well as offering the customary cemetery services, there is a gift shop, café and a woodland nature trail. The cemetery, with its atmosphere of calmness and natural life, is now a popular spot for walks and family outings: very much what was originally envisaged all those years ago.

WHAT TO DO WITH THE DEAD?

The father of modern India

One of the most remarkable monuments in Arnos Vale cemetery is the Hindu-style memorial to Raja Rammohun Roy (1772-1833). Roy was a social reformer, who campaigned, among other issues, against child marriage and sati, the practice of burning widows. Roy was visiting Bristol when he was struck down by cholera and died. He is known as the father of modern India. An annual remembrance service is held on the Sunday nearest his death anniversary, 27 September.

Raja Rammohun Roy was a social reformer, who campaigned, among other issues, against child marriage and sati, the practice of burning widows.

One of the most remarkable monuments in Arnos Vale Cemetery is the Hindu-style memorial to Raja Rammohun Roy (1772-1833).

Holy Souls Roman Catholic Cemetery, Bath Road. Established 1856. Adjoins Arnos Vale Cemetery.

St Mary Redcliffe Burial Ground, Bath Road. Established 1866. Built with money received from the Harbour Railway in compensation for the loss of part of the church's graveyard. Closed 2000.

Greenbank Cemetery, Easton. Established 1871. Extended 1899. In the north eastern section of the cemetery are the memorials to civilians who died during the Bristol Blitz.

Avonview Cemetery, Beaufort Road, St George. A hillside cemetery, established 1883.

Ridgeway Park Cemetery, Eastville. Established by a private company in 1888. Contains a separate area set aside for Jewish burials. The cemetery was also used from 1895 as a burial ground for deceased paupers from the Eastville Workhouse.

Priort to this, the Clifton Union Workhouse in Eastville used a sloping plot of land, **Rosemary Green Graveyard**, behind their buildings as a burial ground. In use from 1851, 4,000 men, women and children from the workhouse were buried here in unmarked graves. The land is now a playing field and park. In 2015 the Bristol Radical History Group unveiled a memorial stone in remembrance of those who lived and died in the Workhouse.

Other Bristol cemeteries include:
- Shirehampton Cemetery, St Mary's Road, established 1898, extended 1907.
- Canford Cemetery, Canford Lane, established 1903.
- Brislington Cemetery, Church Hill, Brislington, established 1905.
- Henbury Cemetery, Kingsweston Road, Henbury. 1923.

Non-conformists had their own burial grounds.

Friend's Burial Ground, Redcliffe Pit. The land was purchased in 1665, closed 1923. Some of the gravestones are still stored in the hermit's cave, dug into the red cliff.

Brunswick Cemetery, Brunswick Square. Established 1768. Originally a 'Presbyterian Burying Ground' it was used by Unitarians in the early nineteenth century. Clark found it 'very neat and clean, turfed and planted'. Since the mid-1980s the cemetery has been used as a public park, known as Brunswick Cemetery Gardens. This slightly unsettling, tucked away park, now contains a series of intriguing cast-iron sculptures by Hew Locke, commissioned in 2009.

Baptist Burial Ground, Redcross Street. Founded 1679, closed 1884. Attached to the Wesleyan Chapel. Now a car park and garden area behind what was once the Central Methodist Hall, Old Market.

Until the provision of purpose-built

Jewish Cemeteries

Queen Elizabeth's Hospital, built on a spur of Brandon Hill and opposite an ancient Mikvah spring, is on the site of an old Jewish graveyard. Many grave stones with Jewish inscriptions were found when the school was erected.[4]

Barton Road, St Philips. This tiny cemetery was established 1740s. Last burial 1944.

Great Gardens, Rose Street, Temple Gate. Established 1811. Purchased by the Great Western Railway in 1913. Rose Street is now under the north east side of Temple Gate roundabout. A number of grave stones were removed and re-erected at the Ridgeway Park Cemetery.

Ridgeway Park, Eastville. Established 1890s. Cemetery in use today. Those buried at this cemetery include: Joseph Abraham, First Jewish Mayor of Bristol in 1865 and Helen (Strimer) Bloom, First Jewish Lord Mayor of Bristol in 1971.

Jewish Cemetery, Barton Road, St Philips. This tiny cemetery was established in the 1740s. Last burial 1944.

crematoriums, cremation was an uncommon and expensive option.

Canford Cemetery opened a crematorium in 1956.

The South Bristol Crematorium, Bedminster Down, was opened in 1971.

In recent years burials have become a popular option in multi-faith cemeteries such as the Memorial Woodlands, at Earthcote in South Gloucestershire.

- Bodies for science -

During the eighteenth century there were not enough cadavers to satisfy the demands of anatomical science.

Helpfully, courts could direct that the body of a condemned man be donated for dissection. In 1755, Catherine Gardener was convicted of the wilful murder of 'her female bastard child'. After hanging 'until she be dead' 'her body was to be Dissected and Anatomised'. Similarly, John Hobbs, who had been convicted of wilful murder in 1758, was sentenced to be hanged and his corpse delivered to Mr Page, the City of Bristol Surgeon for similar morbid research.[5]

Likewise, in 1821, the body of 18-year-old John Horwood, who was convicted for the murder of his girlfriend and publically executed on the roof of the New Gaol by hanging, was delivered to the Bristol Infirmary for dissection. A book giving an account of his trial, on view at the M Shed Museum, was bound with his own tanned skin!

It seems that surgeons were so keen to get their hands on bodies that they rarely asked for provenance. There is an enormous block of stone in the graveyard of Frenchay Village Unitarian Chapel which was placed over newly dug graves to foil the 'resurrectionists'.

In 1821, a 20 guinea reward was offered for information about the theft of 'a corpse out of a grave' from Westbury-on-Trym churchyard. Grave robbing could also be a problem for those of unusual stature. The eight foot tall Bristol Giant, Patrick Cotter (1760 -1806) is said to have had a terror of grave robbers. He died in 1806 and was buried in the Congregational Chapel in Trenchard Street. A 12-foot-deep grave, protected by iron bars, was dug through solid rock to deter exhumation. In spite of these precautions his body was disinterred in 1972, when the Trenchard Street Chapel was demolished to make way for a multi-storey car park. After examination of his remains, it was calculated that Cotter was 246 cms (8ft 1 inch) tall. He was the first of only 13 people known to have surpassed eight feet in height.

Body-snatching was eventually brought under control by the Anatomy Act of 1832 which required teachers of anatomy to be licensed. To make up for the potential lack of cadavers, the Act did, however, give anatomy practitioners official access to unclaimed corpses from hospitals, prisons and workhouses.

ENDNOTES

1. Mason, E. J. *The Horsefair Cemetery, Bristol* in *Transactions of the Bristol and Gloucestershire Archaeological Society* 1957, p.164.
2. Clark, G. T., *Report to the General Board of Health*, 1850, For Her Majesty's Stationery Office. p.17.
3. British Association. *Bristol and its Environs*. 1875, J Wright and Co, p.200.
4. Fedden, M., *Bristol Bypaths*, 1955 (?) Bristol, p.35.
5. Lamoine, G. *Bristol Gaol Delivery Fiats*, Bristol Record Society, 1989. p15.

SOURCES

A Fellow of Queens College in Oxford, *The Sieges of Bristol in the Civil War*, 1868, Lewis and Taylor.
Alexander, J. & Binski, P., (Ed), *Age of Chivalry*, 1987, Royal Academy of Arts.
Anon, *Council House Bristol 1956*, Bristol. Unpaginated commemorative brochure.
Anon., *Bristol and Its Environs*, 1875, London.
Anon., *Bristol Bombed*, 1943, F.G Warne.
Anon., *English City. The Story of Bristol*. 1945, J.S.Frys and Son.
Anon., *How to see Bristol*, 1910, Arrowsmith.
Anon., *The Northern Foul Water Interceptor*, Undated brochure (1994?), Bristol.
Arrowsmith Ltd, *Official Guide to the City of Bristol*, 1921.
Aughton, P., *Bristol – A People's History*, 2003, Carnegie Publishing.
Backwith, D. and Ball, R., *Bread or Batons*, 2012, Bristol Radical History Pamphleteer Pamphlet #19.
Belshaw, G. & Green, R., *Charles Heal and Son's Big Shows*, 2019.
Bennett, J.B., *Bristol of the Future*, 1966.
Bettey, J., *William Worcestre – The Topography of Medieval Bristol*, 2000, Bristol Record Society, Vol. 51.
Bettey, J.H., *The Landscape of Wessex*, 1980, Moonraker Press.
Bettey, J.H., *Bristol Observed*, 1986, Redcliffe Press.
Bishop, J., *Bristol through Maps*, 2016, Redcliffe.
Blackburn, R., *The Overthrow of Colonial Slavery 1776 - 1848*, 1988, Verso.
Bolton, D., *Made in Bristol*, 2011, Redcliffe Press.
Boughton, J., *Municipal Dreams*, 2018, Verso.
Branigan.K., *The Romans in the Bristol Area*, 1969, Bristol Branch of the Historical Association.
Briggs, A., *A Social History of England*, 1983, Weidenfeld and Nicolson.
Bristol City Planning and Public Works Committee, *Bristol of the Future*, 1967, Bristol.
Bristol Times and Mirror, *Work in Bristol*, 1883.
British Association. *Bristol and its Environs*. 1875, J Wright and Co,
Brodie, A., Croom, J. and Davies, J. *Behind Bars*, 1999, English Heritage.
Buchanan, R.A., *The Industrial Archaeology of Bristol*, 1967, Bristol Branch of the Historical Association.
Burton, E. and Manson, M., *Vice and Virtue. Discovering the Story of Old Market*. 2015, Bristol Books.
Clark, G. T., *Report to the General Board of Health*, 1850, For Her Majesty's Stationery Office.
CLASS *Miner's Memories*, 1984?, Adult Studies Department, South Bristol Technical College.
Defoe, D., *A Tour Through the Whole Island of Great Britain*, 1724-6, Penguin edition 1978.
Dening, C.F.W. *Old Inns of Bristol*, 1943, Bristol.
Diaper, S. in Harvey, C. & Press, J., ed., *Studies in the Business History of Bristol*, 1988, Bristol Academic Press.
Dresser, M. & Giles, S. *Bristol and Transatlantic Slavery*, 1999, Bristol Museums and Art Gallery.
Dresser, M., *Black and White on the Buses*, 1986. Bristol Broadsides.

Dresser, M., Jordan, C. & Taylor, D., *Slave Trade Trail*, 1998, Bristol Museums and Art Gallery.
Duffus, J. *The Women Who Built Bristol*, 2018, Tangent.
Duffus, J. *The Women Who Built Bristol: Volume Two*. 2019, Tangent.
Evans, J., *A Chronological Outline of the History of Bristol*, 1824, Bristol.
Fedden, M., *Bristol Bypaths*, 1955, Bristol(?).
Fleming, P. & Costello, K., *Discovering Cabot's Bristol*, 1989, Redcliffe.
Fowler, P.J., *Hill-Forts, A.D. 400 -700*, in ed. Jesson, M. and Hill, D. *The Iron Age and its Hill-Forts,* 1971, University of Southampton.
Foyle, A. & Pevsner, N., *Somerset: North and Bristol*, 2011, Yale University Press.
Foyle, A., *Pevesner Architectural Guides – Bristol, 2004*, Yale University Press.
Franklin, M., *Prisoners of War in Bristol*. Extracts from the Public Records Office, Greenwich, unpublished manuscript, Bristol Central Reference Library, B30152.
Fuller, T., *History of the Worthies of England, Vol. 2*, 1840, London.
Gage, S. in Duffus, J., *The Women Who Built Bristol*, 2018, Tangent.
Ginsell, L.V., *Prehistoric Bristol*. Bristol Branch of the Historical Association, 1969.
Gomme A, Jenner M and Little B: Bristol, *An Architectural History: Bristol*, 1979, Lund Humphries.
Gomme, A. and Jenner, M., *An Architectural History of Bristol,* 2011, Oblong Creative.
Harvey, C. & Press, J., Ed, *Studies in the Business History of Bristol*, 1988, Bristol Academic Press.
Holmes, R., *Coleridge – Darker Reflections*. 1998, Harper Collins.
Horton, B., *West Country Weather Book,* 1995, Bristol.
Hunt, S., *Yesterday's To-morrow*, 2012, Bristol Radical Pamphleteer Pamphlet.
Hutton, S., *Bristol and its Famous Associations*, 1907, Arrowsmith.
Ison, W., *The Georgian Buildings of Bristol*, 1952, Faber & Faber.
Jenner, M., *Bristol's 100 Best Buildings*, 2010, Redcliffe.
Jones, P., *Canon's Marsh – The Rise and Fall of the Tobacco Bonds*, 1988, Redcliffe Press.
Kaufman, M., *Black Tudors*, 2017, One World.
Lambert, D., *Historic Public Parks – Bristol*. 2000, Avon Gardens Trust.
Lamoine, G., *Bristol Gaol Delivery Fiats 1741-1799*, 1989, Bristol Record Society.
Large, D. and Round, F., *Public Health in Mid-Victorian Bristol,* 1944, Bristol Branch of the Historical Association.
Latimer, J., *Annals of Bristol – Seventeenth Century*, 1900, Georges.
Latimer, J., *Annals of Bristol – Eighteenth Century*, 1893, Bristol.
Latimer, J., *Annals of Bristol – Nineteenth Century*, 1887, Bristol.
Legg, R., *Steepholm – Allsop Island*, 1992, Wincanton.
Lindegaard, D.P., *Black Bristolians of the 18th and 19th*

Centuries, self-published, 1990s?
Lock, G. and Relston, I., *Atlas of Hillforts of Britain and Ireland* [On Line]. https://hillforts.arch.ox.ac.uk/
Lord, J. & Southam, J., *The Floating Harbour*, 1983, Redcliffe Press.
Lowery, H., *Bristol Review of Books*, Issue 3, Spring 2007.
Malpass, P. & King, A. *Bristol's Floating Harbour: The First 200 Years.* 2009, Redcliffe.
Malpass, P., *The Bristol Dock Company, 1803 -1848*, 2010, ALHA Booklet,
Manson, M., *Bristol Beyond the Bridge*, 1988, Redcliffe Press.
Manson, M., *Riot! The Bristol Bridge Massacre of 1793*, 1997, Past & Present Press.
Mason, E. J. *The Horsefair Cemetery, Bristol* in *Transactions of the Bristol and Gloucestershire Archaeological Society* 1957.
Matthews, W. Bristol Directory, 1793, Bristol, (facsimile edition).
Merritt, D. & Greenacre, F., *Public Sculpture of Bristol*, 2010, Liverpool University Press.
Morris, J., *Domesday Book – Somerset*, 1980, Phillimore.
Morton, M.V., *In Search of England*, 1929, Methuen and Co.
Moss, F., *City Pit*, 1986, Bristol Broadsides.
Muthesius, S., *The English Terrace House*, 1982, Yale University Press.
Nicholls, J.F. & Taylor,J., *Bristol Past and Present, Volume 1.*1881, Arrowsmith.
Nicholls, J.F. & Taylor, J., *Bristol Past and Present, Volume 2,* 1881, Arrowsmith.
Nichols, G., *Clifton and Durdham Downs: A Place of Public Resort and Recreation*, 2006, Bristol Branch of the Historical Association.
Odery Symes, J., *A Short History of the Bristol General Hospital,* 1932, Bristol.
Ollerenshaw, P., *The Development of Banking in the Bristol Region, 1750-1914*, in Harvey, C. & Press, J., ed. *Studies in the Business History of Bristol*,1988, Bristol Academic Press.
Platt, C., *The English Medieval Town*, 1979, Granada.
Poole, S. & Rogers, N., *Bristol from Below*, 2017, Boydell Press.
Porter, R., *English Society in the Eighteenth Century*, 1990, Penguin Books.
Powell, K.G. *The Marian Martyrs and the Reformation in Bristol*, 1972, Bristol Branch of the Historical Association.
Pudney. J., *Bristol Fashion*, 1960, Putnam.
Quin, P., *The Holy Wells of Bath And Bristol Region*, 1999, Logaston Press.
Ralph, E. *Government of Bristol 1373-1973*, 1973, Bristol Corporation.
Ralph, E., *The Streets of Bristol*, 2001 (Reprint), Bristol Branch of the Historical Association.
Reid, H. *Bristol & Co*, 1987, Redcliffe Press.
Report of the Visiting Justices into the Gaol and Bridewell of the City of Bristol, 1841.
Sanger, 'Lord' G., *Seventy Years a Showman*, 1952, Dent.
Seyer, S., *Memoirs Historical and Topographical of Bristol,* 1823, Bristol.
Sherborne, J., *The Port of Bristol in the Middle Ages,* 1971, Bristol Branch of the Historical Association.
Sherborne, J., *William Canynges 1402-1474.* 1985, Bristol Branch of the Historical Association.
Sketchley's Bristol Directory 1775, Facsimile edition, Kingsmead Reprints.

South Gloucestershire Mines Research Group, *Kingwood Coal,* 2008.
Steeds, M. & Ball, R., *From Wulfstan to Colston,* 2020, Bristol Radical History Group.
Stephenson, P., *Diary of a Black Englishman,* 2011, Tangent Books.
Tratman, E.E., *The Prehistoric Archaeology of the Bristol Region* in *Bristol and Its Adjoining Counties,* 1955, Bristol.
Tout, H., *The Standard of Living in Bristol,* 1938, University of Bristol Social Survey.
Vear, L., *South of the Avon,* 1978, self published, Wotton-Under-Edge.
Vinter, D., *Prisoners of War near Stapleton Road, Bristol.* 1956, Bristol and Gloucester Archaeological Society - Transactions 1956.
Waite, V., *The Bristol Hotwell* in *Bristol in The Eighteenth Century.* 1972, David and Charles.
Walker D., *Bristol in the Early Middle Ages*, 1971, Bristol Branch of the Historical Association.
Walters, W., *The Establishment of the Bristol Police Force*, 1975, Bristol Branch of the Historical Association.
White, K. & Gallop, R., *A Celebration of the Avon New Cut*, 2006, Fiducia Press.
Whitfield, M., *The Bristol Microscopists and the Cholera epidemic of 1849,* 2011, Avon Local History and Archaeology.
Witt,C., *The Bristol Bottlemakers*, 3 June 1978, Chemistry and Industry.
Witt,C., Weedon, C., and Schwind, A.P. *Bristol Glass*, 1984, Redcliffe Press.
Witts, C, *Tales of the River Severn*, 1998.
Wood, J., *A Description of the Exchange of Bristol*, 1745, Bath (Facsimile edition, 1965).
Young, C., *The Making of Bristol's Victorian Parks* in *The Transactions of the Bristol and Gloucestershire Archaeological Society,* Volume 116, 1998.

http://british-police-history.uk/show_nav.cgi?force=bristol_river&tab=0&nav=alpha
https://cardiffharbour.com/flatholm/#1488978342717-6b6c84df-5158
https://cotswoldarchaeology.co.uk/excavation-of-a-roman-villa-complex-in-lockleaze/
https://historicengland.org.uk/listing/the-list/list-entry/1201988
https://historicengland.org.uk/listing/the-list/list-entry/1203910
https://sounds.bl.uk/Accents-and-dialects/Millenium-memory-bank/021M-C0900X00510X-2600V1
https://www.avonandsomerset.police.uk/about/history-of-the-force/
https://www.bbc.co.uk/history/ww2peopleswar/stories/60/a5382560.shtml
https://www.countyasylums.co.uk/barrow-hospital-barrow-gurney/
https://www.countyasylums.co.uk/history/
https://www.merchantventurers.com/
https://www.slavevoyages.org/
https://www.ucl.ac.uk/lbs/person/view/45909 Legacies of Slave Ownership database.

I must give a special mention to the digital mapping website, *Know Your Place*. Rarely a day of writing went by without consulting this magnificent and visionary resource.

ACKNOWLEDGEMENTS

When I started writing local history in the 1980s academics were strangely condescending about the topic. I was surprised. To me local history is real history, featuring the place I live in. It wasn't about remote kings and queens – it was about everyday people within a familiar landscape.

Fortunately, all that has changed. In the 1990s I attended Bristol Polytechnic (now UWE) to study for a Post Graduate Diploma in Local Studies. At last, local history was being taken seriously. I was fortunate to be taught by such luminaries as Madge Dresser, Peter Fleming and Steve Poole. Fellow students included Jonathon Harlow and Mike Hooper. There was an infectious enthusiasm for this new subject that was at last being taken seriously: working class history; women's history; a forensic analysis of the slave trade were all to the fore.

Now we have the *Regional Studies Centre*, the heroic *Bristol Radical History Group*, the *Avon Local History and Archaeology* group and the one woman powerhouse Jane Duffus. In my head I hear Jane urging me: 'where are the women?' And I know I have failed miserably on this count – there is always more to be done. Meanwhile, the *Radicals* continue to spotlight working-class history and the legacy of slavery, initiating ground-breaking research and challenging commonly held ideas.

We are also fortunate in Bristol that we have resources to hand. We are blessed with the miles of books and research already undertaken on our unique city. Every time I visit Bristol Archives I marvel that we have access to such treasures. The same goes to Bristol Reference Library. And, of course, these places are staffed by the most knowledgeable people.

We've also been privileged in Bristol to have some great publishers. It is largely thanks to them that Bristol's history has been made so accessible. In the last 40 years John and Angela Sansom's Redcliffe Press has led the way. It's due to the encouragement of Redcliffe that I started writing history, in fact writing at all. Their 200-plus books on Bristol are an impressive memorial to John Sansom who sadly passed away in 2019.

We are fortunate to have so many passionate experts ready to share their knowledge and learning. Many people have helped and advised me on this project. Academics, historians, dilettantes and interested individuals have all offered information and advice. In no particular order I would like to thank them for so generously contributing time, expertise and enthusiasm: Professors Steve Poole, Madge Dresser and Peter Fleming for leading the way; Roger Ball and comrades from the Bristol Radical History Group for keeping it real; the inspirational Jane Duffus whose recent books have brought Bristol's women out of the shadow; the fabled Richard Jones, unflagging supporter of creative endeavours in Bristol; Dr Jonathon Harlow for his thoughts on the everyday workings of Bristol harbour; Roy Gallop of Fiducia Press; erudite pub landlord and author, Mark Steeds; the indomitable Ruth Hecht; Trevor Coombs from the Museum and Art Gallery for his support and advice with regards illustrations; Eugene Byrne from the *Bristol Post* – a mine of information, always beautifully told; the eminent Dr Edson Burton and Stella Man for information about Glenside and the history of psychiatric care.

Also: the celebrated Tangent Lunch club – Richard Jones, Beccky Golding, Andy Hamilton, Mark Steeds, Jo Darke and Nicky Coates for mental sustenance (and laughter).

On the creative writing side I've had on-going encouragement and advice from the brilliant and dynamic Bristol Writers Group: Andy Hamilton, Corrine Dobinson, Gavin Watkins, Justin Newland, Piers Marter, Ray Newman, Sarah Thorne and Tony Northover.

The *Bristol Miscellany* has only see the light of day thanks to the vision and enthusiasm of the Bristol Books Team. My heartfelt thanks to Joe Burt, Clive Burlton, Martin Powell and Richard Jones (again!).

And most important of all, my love, life-force and fellow explorer, Maggie Moss. Maggs, this is for you.

INDEX

Bold italics indicate an illustration

Abonae, 11, **11**
Abraham, Joseph, 145
Acraman's Anchor Works, 133
Aeroplane industry, 62
Aethelred the Unready, 32
Africans in Bristol, 96
Airbus Jumbo Jet A300, 86
All Saints Lane, 77
Almondsbury, 96
American Consulate, **96**, 97
American GIs, 82
American War of Independence, 99
Anatomy Act (1832), 146
Aqua Sulis (Bath), 11
Arnos Court, 30
Artspace Lifespace, 50
Ashley Hill, 120
Ashley Vale, 12
Ashton, 90, 107, 111
Avon Gorge, 10, **102**, 111, 121, 129
Avon New Cut – see New Cut.
Avonmouth, 102
Avonmouth Docks, 88, 122

Badocks Wood, 9
Bailey, Guy, 63, 64
Baldwin Street, 70
Bantock, Anton, 141
Barrow Gurney, 122, 137, 138
Barton Hill, 31, 95
Bath, 31, 76
Baths and washhouses, 119, **119**
Bathurst Basin, 99**, 101**, 102, 133, 135
Bathurst, Sir Charles, 102
Bay of Biscay, 71
Bazalgette, Joseph, 118
Beaconsfield, Bucks, 37
Beaufort War Hospital, 137
Beddoes, Dr Thomas, 112
Bedminster, 13, 107, 115, 116, 118, 133
Bedminster Down, 12, 122, 141
Benn MP, Tony, 64
Berkeley Square, 25
Bird's Eye tobacco, 89
Birmingham, 81
Bishop's Palace, looting of, 59
Bishop's Knoll, lost gardens, 127
Black Death, 109
Black Lives Matter, 96, **96**

Black Rock spring, 121
Blackwell, Dr Elizabeth, 139, **139**
Blagdon Reservoir, 122
Blaise Castle folly, 11
Blaise Castle House, 97
Blanket, Thomas, 71
Bloom, Helen, 145
BMW, 85
Bordeaux, 71
Botanic Gardens, University of Bristol, 130
Bragg, Christopher, 43
Brandon Hill, 29, 120
Brentry, 20
Bridge Valley Road, 111
Bristol Bridge, 20, 71, 75, **77**
Bristol Bridge, riot (1793), 47
Bridgwater, 70
Brislington House Asylum, 138
Brislington Roman Villa, 11-12
Brislington Tram Depot, 91
Bristol Aeroplane Company, 86
Bristol Beacon (formerly Colston Hall), 120
Bristol Blue Glass, 91, **92**
Bristol Boats, 84
Bristol Books, 84
Bristol Brabazon, 86, **87**
Bristol Bullet, 85
Bristol Cars, 85, **85, 86**
Bristol, cathedral city, 22
Bristol Cigarettes, 89, **89**, 90
Bristol City Council, 63
Bristol, coat of arms, 26, **26**
Bristol, county status, 20, 28
Bristol Cream, 88, **88, 89**
Bristol Dispensary, 131, 132
Bristol Harbour, 99-102
Bristol Lodekka Bus, 91, **91**
Bristol Medical Mission, 131
Bristol Milk, 88
Bristol Mirror, 118
Bristol Museum and Art Gallery, 81
Bristol Museum: M Shed, 91
Bristol Omnibus Company, 63
Bristol Pneumatic Institute, 112, **122**
Bristol, Port of, 69-70,
Bristol Radical History Group, 143
Bristol Scroll, 84, **84**
Bristol Tramways Company, 67
Bristol Union Workhouse, 136
Bristol Water Company, 122

British and Colonial Aeroplane Company, 84
British Leyland, 91
British Museum, 73
Broad Street, 109
Broad Street, 25, 60, 65, 109
Broad Weir, 43
Bronze Age, 9
Brooks:
- Ashton Brook, 15
- Beg Brook, 15
- Brislington Brook, 15
- Colliters Brook, 15
- Coombe Brook, 16
- Cranbrook, 16
- Cutlers Mill Brook, 16, 125
- Fishponds Brook, 16
- Hazel Brook, 15
- Henry Sleed Stream, 16
- Horfield Brook, 15, 16, 125
- Longmore Brook, 16
- Malago, 17, 102
- Pigeon House Stream, 17
- The Danny, 15
- Wain Brook, 17, **17**
Brunswick Cemetery Gardens, 124
Brunswick Square, 123
Burgh Walls, 10
Burke, Edmund, 37, **37**
Bus Boycott, 63-4, **63**
Butlin, Billy, 83
Bye laws, 42

Cabot, John, 34, **69**, *120*
Cabot, Sebastian, 120
Cameron Balloons, 84
Canon's Marsh, 90
Canynges family, 72
Canynges, William the Younger, 72-4, **74**
Cardiff Harbour Authority, 23
Caribbean, 93
Carty, Peter, 64
Castle Park, 28, 43
Castle, Bristol, 14, 20, 27-8, **27, 28**, 56
Cattelena, 96
Chaney, Jonathan, 46
Charles II, 44
Charlton Village, 86, 87
Chepstow Castle, 56
Chester, 32

153

Chew Valley Reservoir, 122
Cholera, 115-6, 118, 122, 133
Churches:
- St John's, 120
- All Saints, 43
- Cotham Parish, 46
- St James's, 117
- St Jude's 115
- St Mary Redcliffe, 29, 56, 72, 73, **73** 80, **116**, 120,
- St Nicholas, 117
- St Thomas's, 76, 79
- Temple, 19, **19**, 99
City Hall (formerly Council House), 34-6, **34**, **35, 36**
Civil War, 29
Clark, G. T., 116-7
Clifton Down, 128
Clifton Down Road, 10
Clifton Down Station, 82
Clifton Observatory, 9, 121
Clifton Suspension Bridge, 84
Clifton, 13, 30, 118, 121
Coach and Horses, Gloucester Lane, 83
Coal:
- Ashton Vale, 107, 108
- Bedminster Pit, 104,
- Coalpit Heath, **103**, 104, 107, 108
- Dean Lane Pit, 104, 107, 108
- Deep Pit, **106**, 108
- Easton Colliery, **107, 108**, 108
- Extent of the coal field, 103
- Frog Lane Pit, **105**
- Hanham Colliery, 107
- Harry Stoke Pit, 108
- Kilmersdon, 108
- Long Ashton Pit, **104**
- Malago Vale Pit, 104, 108
- Miner's wages, 107
- Parkfield Colliery, **106**, 107, 108
- Shortwood Lodge, 108
- South Liberty Pit, 107, 108
- Speedwell Pit, **105**, 108
- Writhlington, 108
Coins, 13
Coins, forgery, 45
Coleridge, Samuel Taylor, 112
College Green, 24, 34, 123, 125
Colman, Samuel, 81
Colston Avenue, 125
Colston Hall, see Bristol Beacon
Colston, Edward, 7, 94, 95
Colston, Statue, **96**
Combe Dingle, 12
Community Care, 137
Concorde, 84

Corn Exchange, 76-7, **76, 77**
Corn Street, 25, 60, 79
Cornwallis House, 97
Cotham Gardens, 125
Cotter, Patrick, 146
Council House, 60, 66
County Asylum Act (1808), 136
Courts:
- Court of Assize, 41
- Court of the Admiralty, 41
- Court of the Mayor and Sheriff, 41
- Court Pie Poudre, 41, **42**
- Tolzey, 41
- Quarter Sessions, 41
- Staple Court, 41
Cowlin and Son, 36
Cramner, Thomas, 46
Crews Hole Copper Works, 30
Crimean Campaign, 124
Crisp, Henry, 48
Cromwell, Oliver, 28
Cross, Mary, 43
Crosses:
- Bewell's Cross, 25
- Don John's Cross, 25
- High Cross, 24-25, **24**, **25,** 75, 76
- Old Market Cross, 25
- Red Cross, 25
- St Peter's Cross, 25
- Stallage Cross, 25
Crown Insurance Fire Office, 66
Cumberland Basin, 99, **100**
Curtis, Bill, 62
Cutler, Adge, 17

Davies, D., 122
Davy, Humphrey, 104, 112, 113
Davy Safety Lamp, 104, 107, 112
De La Beche, Sir Henry, 116
Dead Horse Lane, 117
Deadalus, HMS, 124
Defoe, Daniel, 70, 76, 103, 111
Demerara, SS, 101
Denny Island, **23**
Devizes, 72
Dock Company, 99, 100
Domesday Book, 13
DoubleTree Hilton, 92
Downs, The, 11, 111, 121, 122, 123,128-9, **128**
Dr Who, 49, 90
Dundry, 15, 17, 141
Durdham Down, 123, 128

Easton, 107
Eastville Workhouse, 137, 143

Edgelands:
- Callington Road Nature Reserve, 127
- Easter Garden, Wesley Place, 127
- Hartcliffe Millennium Green, 127
- Narroways, 127
- Northern Slopes, 127
Edward I, 26
Edward II, 41
Edward III, 19
Edward IIII, 28
Elmina Castle, Cape Coast, 93
Elizabeth I, 24, 96
Elton, Sir Abraham, 91
Exeter, 32

Fairs:
- Durdham Down Fair, 82
- Redcliffe Fair, 80
- St George's Park Fair, **82**
- St James's Fair, 80, **80**, 81, **81** 110
- St Paul's Fair, 80
Temple Street Fair, 81
Fairfax, John, 9
Fairfax, Michael, 9
Fairground Heritage Centre, 83
Ferguson, George, 36
Filton, 86
Fire Service, 65-7, **65**, **66, 67**
First World War, 137
Flat Holm, 20, 23
Floating Harbour, 100, 101
Florence Nightingale, 134, 139
Forest of Dean, 107
Fox, Edward Long, 138
Fox's Book of Martyrs, 46
French Prisoners, 100
French's Yard, 56
Frenchay Village Unitarian Chapel, 146
Frome Valley, 118

Gardener, Catherine, 145
Gas Lamps, 55
Gascony, 71, 73
Gateways:
- Back Gate, 29
- Castle Gate, 29
- Lawfords Gate, 29, 30, 100
- Redcliffe Gate, 29
- St John's Gate, **30**, 31
- Temple Gate, 29, **29**
Georgian House, 97
Gingell, William, Bruce, 135
Glassworks, 92
Glastonbury, 82

INDEX

Glenside, 137
Glenside Hospital Museum, 138
Gloucester, 14, 72
Gloucestershire, 20, 23, 28
Gloucester Lane, 83
Goldney House, 97
Gomme and Jenner, 33
Graveyards and cemeteries:
- Arnos Vale, 142, **142**
- Avonview Cemetery, 143
- Baptist's Burial Ground, 144
- Body-snatching, 145
- Brunswick Cemetery, 144, **144**
- Crematoriums, 145
- Christchurch, 142
- Friends Burial Ground, 144
- Greenbank Cemetery, 143
- Jewish Cemeteries, 145, **145**
- Ridgeway Park Cemetery, 143
- Roman cemeteries, 141,
- Rosemary Green Graveyard, 143
- St Mary Redcliffe Burial Ground, 143

Great Britain, SS, 101
Great Ditch, 29
Great Drought (1976), 122
Great Exhibition (1851), 24
Great Fire of London, 65
Great George Street, 33, 94
Great Re-coinage, 32
Great Red Book, 22
Great Western Cotton Factory, 95
Great Western Railway, 94
Great Western, 101
Guinea Street, 133, 135

Hackett, Roy, **63**, 64
Handbook for the Instruction of Attendants on the Insane, 136
Harford, Joseph, 38
Harris, E Vincent, 25, 34
Hartcliffe, 20, 90
Harvey & Sons, John, 88
Heal & Son, Charles, 82, **82, 83**
Health Research Institute, University of Bristol, 139
Helluland, 72
Henbury churchyard, 94
Hengrove Park, 15
Henry II, 28
Henry III, 70
Henry VI, 28
Henry VII, 24
Henry VIII, 20, 22, 28, 46, 74, 110
Henry, Owen, 64
Heresy, 46
High Street, 45, 109

Hillfort, Blaise Castle, 11
Hobbs, John, 145
Hodgkin, Dorothy, 135
Home Office, 55
Horfield Common, 125
Horfield Gardens, 55
Horse Races, **128**, 129
Horwood, John, 54, 145
Hospitals:
- Beaufort War Hospital, 137
- Cossham Hospital, 132
- Bristol Dispensary, 131, 132
- Bristol Eye Hospital, 132
- Bristol General Hospital, 132, 133-5, **133, 134**
- Bristol Homeopathic Hospital, 132
- Bristol Infirmary, 133, 146
- Bristol Mental Hospital, 137
- Bristol Royal Infirmary, **131**, 132
- South Bristol Community Hospital, 135

Hotel Bristol, 84
Hotwell Road, 78
Hotwell Water, 111
Hotwell, 31, 129, 111
House Tax, 32
Houston, Libby, 129
Hundred Years War, 71
Hungroad, 69
Hunt, William, 125

Iberian Peninsula, 71, 73
Iceland, 71, 73
Imperial Tobacco Group, 89
Imports, wine, 71
Inns Court Farm, 12
Ireland, 14
Iron Age, 9
Isca Silurum (Caerleon), 11

Jacobite Rebellion, 30
Jacobs Wells Road, 122
Jacobs, Issac, 91, **92**
Jeffreys, Judge, 44-5
Jessop, William, 99
John Cabot, 72
Jones, Pero, 94

Kenneth Allsop Memorial Trust, 23
Keynsham Abbey, 22
King Square, 123
King, Dr Martin Luther, 64
King's Down, 31
King's Weston Hill, 10
King's Weston Villa, 12
King's Wood, 30

Kingroad, 69
Kings Weston House, 97
Kingswood, 107
Klima, Ivan, 7
Knights Templar, 19
Knowle, 13

Ladies Mile, 129
Latrines, 117
Law Ditch, 117
Lawrence Hill, 31, 110
Lawrence Weston, 11, 20
Leigh Court, 97
Leland, John, 28
Leprosy, 110
Lewis's Department Store, 141
Line of Works, 122
Little Red Book, 22
Liverpool, 38, 99, 116
Llandoger Trow, 14, **14**
Lloyds Bank, 90
Lock's Yard, Bedminster, 83
Lockleaze, roman villa, 12, **12**
London, 13, 38, 81
Long John Silver, 84
Lords of the Manor of Henbury, 128
Lucky Lane, 117
Lunacy Act (1845), 136
Lunatic Asylum, Bristol, 136
Lunatic Asylum, Stapleton, 136, 137, **137**

M Shed Museum, 146
Maby, Chief Constable, 60, 61, 62
Madhouse Act (1774), 136
Mansion House:
- Elmdale, 33, **33**, 39
- looting of, 59
- Queen Square, 33, **33**
Maps:
- Millerd's, 76
- William Smith's, 31, **31**
- Marconi, Guglielmo, 23
Mariners Drive, 11
Markes, Robert, 45
Markets:
-Broadmead, 75
- Farmers, 79
- Fish, 75, 117
- St Nicholas, **76**, 77
- Philips Marsh, 78
- Temple Meads, 78
- Temple Street, 75
- Thomas Street, 75, 76, 78
Marley, Bob, 96
Mary, Queen, 46
Matilda, Queen, 28

155

Matthew, 26, **70**, 72
Matthews, William, 92, 121
McFall, David, 34
Members of Parliament, 36
Mendips, 23, 122
Merchant Venturers, Society of, 38-9, **38**, 121, 123
Merchant's Hall, 39
Mikveh, 122, 145
Milltut Field, 9
Milton, William, 99, 100
Minehead, 70
Mint, 28, 32, **32**
Monmouth, Duke of, 44
Monnington, W.T., 36
Morris, Sarah, 46

Nails, The, 76, 79, **79**
National Board of Health, 116
National Health Service, 131
National Unemployed Workers Union, 60
Navvies, 100
Naylor, James, 46, **46**
Netham Lock, 15
New Cut, 54, 100, 101, 118, 135,
Nightingale Valley, 10, 15
Normans, 27
North America, 72, 93
Northwoods House, Winterbourne, 138
Norton's Mansion, 32
Norwich, 32

Oatley and Thomas, 135
Oatley, George, 48, 132
Old Market, 28, **28**, 117
Old Market Street, 28, 29, 60, 62, 75, 78
On the Buses, 91
Orchard Street, 116

Page, City of Bristol Surgeon, 145
Park Street, 29
Parks:
 - Ashton Court Estate, 124
 - Badocks Wood, 124
 - Brandon Hill, 123, **123**, 124,
 - Dame Emily, 125
 - Eastville, 124, 125
 - Greville Smythe, 125
 - Hengrove, 124
 - Mina Road, 125
 - Montpelier, 125
 - Old Sneed, 127, **127**
 - Redcliffe Hill, 126
 - Sparke Evans, 126

- St Andrews, **124**, 126
- St George's, 107, 126
- St Matthias', 126
- Victoria, 124, 125
- Victory, 126
Peel, Robert, 47
Pero Jones, 94
Picton Street – lock-up, **51**
Pilkingtons, 92
Pill, pilots of, 69
Pinney, Charles, 94
Pinney, John, 94
Pitch and Pay Lane, 110
Plague, 109-110, 141
Plague Pits, 141
Police:
 - Avon & Somerset Constabulary 50
 - Dogs, 48, **48**
 - lack of, 59
 - Mounted Section, 48
 - River Police, 48
 - Uniform, **47**
 - Women, **47**, 48
Police Stations:
 - Bedminster, 47, 48, **49**
 - Bridewell, 49, **49**, 50, 60
 - Central 47
 - Clifton, 47
 - Horfield, 48
 - Redland, 48
 - Rupert Street, 50
 - St George, 48
 - Wine Street, 47, 48
Pope, Alexander, 111
Portishead, 102, 111
Portland Square, 123
Portsmouth, 56
Portugal, 12, 71
Portwall, 29, 30, 71
Portway, 12
Powell, Enoch, 137
Prewett Street, 92
Prince of Wales (1901), 88
Prince Rupert, 29
Prisoners of war, 56
Prisons:
 - Horfield, 45, 55-6,
 - Knowle, 56
 - Lawfords Gate, **53, 58**
 - Newgate, 43, 45, **52**, 136
 - Old Bridewell, 48
 - French Prison, 136
 - New Gaol, 53-5, **54, 55**, 145
Proctor, Thomas, 33
Proctor's Walk, 126
Prussia, 71, 73

Psychiatric care, 136-8, **137**
Public Health Act (1848), 123
Public Health Act (1984), 116
Public Health, 115-9
Punishment:
 - Burning, **44**, 46
 - Ducking Stool, 43
 - Gallows, 44, 45
 - Public Executions, 54
 - Stocks, 43, **44**
 - Transportation, 45
 - Whipping, 43, **43**
Pyronaut, 67

Quakers, 38
Quay, The, 71
Quay Head, 65
Quay Pipe, 120
Queen Square, 29, 33, 58, 96, 97, 123, 133

Race Relations Act (1965), 64
Rare plants, 129
Redcliffe, 19, 29, 70
Redcliffe Back, 73
Redcliffe Caves, 56
Redcliffe Hill, 29, 43, 45
Redcliffe Meads, 30
Redcliffe sand, 92
Redcliffe Street, 43
Reeve, William, 30
Report to the Central Board of Health (1850), **117**
Riots:
 - Riots, 57
 - 1831, 47, **57, 59**
 - Bristol Bridge, (1793), 47, 59
 - Old Market, (1932), 60 62, **61**
 - Queen Square (1831), 58, **58**, 59
Rivers:
 - Avon, 10, **14**, 15, 19, 20, 29, 69, 101, 117, 120, 121
 - Bristol Channel, 70
 - Frome, 15, 16, 29, 43, 70, 117, 120
 - Severn, 14, **14**, 20, 69, 70, 72, 122
 - Wye, 14, 72
 - Yeo, 122
Rogers, H.E., 60
Rolinda Sharples, 128, 129
Romans, 11-2, 13
Roman Way, 11
Rowe, William, 45
Rownham Meads Ferry, 111
Roy, Raja, Rammohun, 143, **143**
Royal African Company, 38, 94
Royal Commission on the Health of Towns (1845), 123

INDEX

Royal Fort, 97, **97**
Royal Institution, London, 112
Rubbish collection, 118
Rummer, The, 77
Rural Dean of the Diocese of Bristol, 117

Sandham Memorial Chapel, 137
Saxton, William, 46
Scarlet Lychnis, 130, **130**
Scipio Africanus, 94, **95**
Sea Mills, 11, 12
Second World War, 34, 67, 82, 85, 102, 135
Sedgemoor, 44
Seven Sisters, 10
Seyer, Samuel, 10
Sheffield, 81
Shrewsbury, 14
Silk Road, 71
Slave Ship, **93**
Slave trade, see Transatlantic slave trade
Slavery, abolition, 94
Slavery, compensation, 94
Slider, The, 10
Smallpox, 110
Smiles Brewery, 84
Smyth, Dame Emily, 107
Smyths, of Ashton Court, 107
Social Science Congress (1869), 139
Somerset judgement (1772), 94
Somerset, 20, 23
South Bristol, 89
South Gloucestershire Gazette, 61
South Wales, 72, 107
Southampton, 109
Southey, Robert, 81, 112
Spain, 71
Spanish Prisoners, 56
Spencer, Stanley, 137
St Anne's Holy Well, 22, **22**
St Anne's Wood, 15
St George, 107
St John's Hospital, 120
St Michael's Hill, 29, 132
St Michael's Parish, 110
St Pauls, 117
St Peter's Hospital, 32, **32**
St Peter's Workhouse, 136, 137, 147
St Philips's, 115, 118
St Thomas Parish, 19
Stag and Hounds, 41, **42**
Stapleton, 56
Stapleton Workhouse, 56
Steep Holm, 20, 23
Stephen, King, 28

Stephenson OBE, Paul, 64
Stockwood, 20
Stoke Bishop, 11
Stoke Park Colony, 138
Stokeleigh Camp, 10
Stourhead Park, 24
Streams – see Brooks
Suffolk, 91
Sugar plantations, 93
Swain, Mary, 43
Sweating Sickness, 110

Temple, 19, 20, 29
Temple Street, 94, 120
Tewkesbury, 14, 81
The Island, 50
Thomas Street, 30, 32
Thornbury Castle, 110
Three Castles tobacco, 89
Tobacco plantations, 93
Toilets, 115
Toll Gates, burning of, 57
Tolzey, 76, **78**, 79
Transatlantic slave trade, 38, 39, 93-7
Transport and General Workers Union, 64
Treen Mill, 13
Trenchard Street, 146

Underwood, Charles, 142
Unemployment, 62
Upper Belgrave Road, 128
Upper Maudlin Street, 12

Varney, Reg, 91
Via Julia, 11, **11**
Victoria, Queen, 36
Vikings, 72

Walcombe Slade, 128
Wallace and Gromit, 84
Walls, 29-31, 71
  - Portwall, 29, 30, 71
Walsall, 81
Watchet, 70
Water supply, 120-3, **120, 121, 122**
Waterloo Street, 117
Watershed, 79
Watt, James, 112
Welfare State, 131
Welsh Back, 71
West Indies, 93
Westbury College, 74
Westbury-on-Trym, 146
Weston-super-Mare, 23
Whapping Wharf, 55

Wheeler, Charles, 34
White Tree, The, 129
Whiteladies Road, 122
Wilberforce, William, 38
William III, 32
Wills, W.D. & H.O., 89, 132
Wills, W.H., 37
Wills, Walter Melville, 132
Wilson, Harold, 64
Winchester, 13
Window Tax, 32
Witchcraft Act (1601), 46
Withywood, 20
Wood, John, 76
Woollen cloth trade, 71
Worcester, William of, 22, 73, 111, 120
Wulfstan, Bishop of Worcester, 71

York, 32

MANSON'S BRISTOL MISCELLANY

PICTURE CREDITS

Unless otherwise stated, photographs and illustrations are from the author's collection. We are most grateful to the Bristol Post and Bristol Culture and Creative Industries for permission to use images from their collections.

The Illustrations, maps and images kindly provided by Bristol Archives are noted opposite along with their respective catalogue Reference Numbers. Although reproduction permission for most rests with Bristol City Council, it has not been possible to determine the copyright status for all of the images reproduced.

p26 top, RefNo: CC/3/3
p26 bottom, RefNo: PicBox/5/doc/64
p31 RefNo: PicBox/6/map/11b
p33 middle, RefNo: PicBox/2/bbg/95
p35 top, RefNo: PicBox/4a/chf/31
p35 bottom, RefNo: PicBox/4a/chf/170
p37 RefNo: PicBox/6/port/6/1
p42 RefNo: 40826/CER/14/1
p47 RefNo: 40826/POL/001
p48 RefNo: 40826/POL/004
p53 RefNo: Postcards/87/1
p58 bottom, RefNo: PicBox/5/evpic/10
p65 RefNo: 17563/1/842
p66 RefNo: 43207/20/3/31
p67 bottom, RefNo: 43207/20/3/3
p85 RefNo: 40826/MOT/3
p86 RefNo: PicBox/5/ind/18/7
p87 top, PicBox/1/air/14/18
p87 bottom, RefNo: PicBox/1/air/14/26
p88 RefNo: 40826/IND/5/2
p89 left, RefNo: 40826/IND/5/9
p89 right, RefNo: 40826/IND/5/7
p90 RefNo: PicBox/5/ind/18/6
p105 top, RefNo: PicBox/4/Coal/4b
p105 bottom, RefNo: PicBox/4/Coal/7b
p106 top, RefNo: PicBox/4/Coal/1a
p106 bottom, RefNo: PicBox/4/Coal/5b
p119 RefNo: 43207/1/32
p123 RefNo: 43207/11/18
p134 RefNo: 43207/9/37/61

THE AUTHOR

Michael Manson studied sociology at Leicester University. He has an MA in Creative Writing from Bath Spa University and a Post Graduate Diploma from Bristol Polytechnic in Local Studies.

Michael was a co-editor of the *Bristol Review of Books* (2006-13), a co-founder of the Bristol Short Story Prize (2008) and is an organiser of the Bristol Festival of Literature (2010 to present). He currently edits Bristol Civic Society's magazine *Better Bristol*.

Michael is the author of four history books on Bristol:

- *Bristol Beyond the Bridge* (Redcliffe)
- *Riot! The Bristol Bridge Massacre of 1793* (Tangent Books)
- *The Hidden History of St Andrews* (Past & Present Press)
- *Vice and Virtue. Discovering the Story of Old Market, Bristol* (with Dr Edson Burton) (Bristol Books)

Mike has also written three novels. In 2015 his Bristol-based novel *Where's My Money*? was selected by BBC TV as one of their *Books that Made Britain*. The *Jamaica Gleaner* described Mike's recent novel, *Down in Demerara*, as 'story telling at its best'.

© Paul Bullivant

COMING SOON!

MANSON'S BRISTOL MISCELLANY VOLUME 2

To include:

- **Getting around** – roads, ferries, trams, trains and bridges.
- **Webs of communication** – newspapers and telecommunications.
- **Earth, wind and flood** – weather extremes and earthquakes.
- **Realists and romantics** – a new poetic movement, literary connections.
- **A roof over your head** – almshouses, workhouses, orphanages and social housing.
- **Buildings of Bristol** – bricks and stones, grand houses, squares, windmills and post war reconstruction.

And so much more...